Growing Hardy Orchids

NO POSTAGE
NECESSARY
IF MAILED
IN THE
UNITED STATES

BUSINESS REPLY MAIL
FIRST CLASS MAIL PERMIT NO. 717 PORTLAND, OR

POSTAGE WILL BE PAID BY ADDRESSEE

TIMBER PRESS, INC.
The Haseltine Building
133 S.W. Second Avenue, Suite 450
Portland, OR 97204-9743

Thank you for choosing this Timber Press book. Our books are widely available at good bookstores and garden centers.

To receive our free catalog or e-mail announcements, complete and return this card, or visit our Web site at: **www.timberpress.com/rr**

Name (please print) _____

Address _____

City _____ State _____ Zip _____

E-mail address _____

❑ I prefer not to receive e-mail announcements.　　❑ Do not share this information with any other company or organization.

We'd also welcome your comments on this book.

Title of book _____

How did you hear about this book? _____

Comments _____

_____

_____

_____

TIMBER PRESS

GROWING
HARDY ORCHIDS

John Tullock

TIMBER PRESS
PORTLAND • LONDON

Photographs by author unless otherwise noted. Frontispiece: *Platanthera psycodes*.

Published in 2005 by
Timber Press, Inc.

The Haseltine Building
133 S.W. Second Avenue, Suite 450
Portland, Oregon 97204-3527
www.timberpress.com

2 The Quadrant
135 Salusbury Road
London NW6 6RJ
www.timberpress.co.uk

Printed in China

Second printing 2008

Library of Congress Cataloging-in-Publication Data

Tullock, John.
  Growing hardy orchids / by John Tullock.
    p. cm.
  Includes bibliographical references and index.
  ISBN-13: 978-088192-715-3 (hardback)
  1. Orchid culture. 2. Orchids. I. Title.
  SB409.T8485 2005
  639.9′344—dc22   2004015599

A catalog record for this book is also available from the British Library.

For Jerry & Sam

Contents

Preface

ABJURE CHALLENGE, AND LIFE LOSES RICHNESS AND texture. The acceptance of a challenge inspired this book. I began, many years ago, learning how to grow hardy terrestrial orchids. Initially I wanted to cultivate as many species as possible of the orchids native to the Great Valley of the Tennessee River. So much of what I'd read about these plants suggested it could not be done. I could not figure out why that might be, since as a biology student I had learned that the local orchids were not fundamentally different from other plants and indeed were tougher than many.

Margie Hunter, in her excellent book, *Gardening with the Native Plants of Tennessee* (2002), points out that including native plants in designed landscapes creates "a sense of place." That sense of place infuses this book. While the discussion mostly covers growing the many kinds of orchids that are hardy outdoors in the temperate zone, my views regarding the conservation of wild plants, the importance of maintaining biodiversity, and the role of the individual as preservationist all receive attention. I am lucky to be a trained naturalist living

9

amid the rich biodiversity of the Tennessee Valley. I developed my orchid growing techniques through direct observation of numerous orchid species in their natural settings, observations accumulated over thirty years of excursions up and down the valley and into the mountains on either side of it. Assisted by the insights of other orchidists whose works appear in the bibliography, I now grow twelve North American orchid species and three exotic ones. Many of these plants have been in my garden for years and have produced numerous offspring.

This book includes a compilation of the work of numerous hardy orchid enthusiasts, supplemented by data gleaned from my own notebooks. I do not claim to have grown every plant described. Gardening may be likened to politics in the context of Tip O'Neill's famous assertion that all politics is local. The growing conditions available to American gardeners vary widely, and microhabitats exist even within the confines of a single backyard. Every state, however, has native orchids, and exotic species exist with horticultural requirements that can be accommodated somewhere—if not in my garden, then perhaps in yours.

Acknowledgments

This book would not have been possible without the kind cooperation of hardy orchid fanciers and biologists throughout North America. Jeff Becker, Paul Martin Brown, Joe Caldwell, Dick "Red" Cavender, Bill Cullina, Scott Durkee, Barry Glick, Rodd May, Ned Nash, Tom Nelson, Wilford Neptune, William Steele, Carson Whitlow, and Gene Wofford all kindly shared their time and expertise. Among my ichthyological colleagues, Gerry Dinkins, David Etnier, Pat Rakes, J. R. and Peggy Shute, and Bob Stiles have shared many good times and good discussions with me, for which I shall always be deeply grateful.

Information about plant conservation regulations and their enforcement came from Claude Bailey, Dick Biggins, Bob Hatcher, Jim Herrig, Jim Keener, Keith Langdon, Carl Nordman, and Lynn Snodderly. In addition, officials of Tennessee State Parks, Great Smoky Mountains National Park, and Big South Fork National River and Recreation Area, too numerous to mention, always offered help and advice on finding orchids in the wild, and did so with good cheer and courtesy.

Tom Mirenda of the Smithsonian Institution and James Newbern of the University of Tennessee Horticulture Gardens offered insight and provided assistance in locating growers and experts.

Special thanks are due to Manuel Aubron, Jack Carman, Dick Cavender, Global Book Publishing, Susan (Mrs. Philip) Keenan, W. George Schmid, and J. R. Shute for the use of their excellent photographs, and to David Boruff and Paulo Reis for their digital graphics expertise. Thanks, too, to Dick Cavender for his helpful comments on the catalog section.

None of these individuals should be considered to share the views expressed in this book. Further, any errors in the interpretation of their work are mine alone.

Finally, I'd like to thank my agent, Grace Freedson, and Timber Press executive editor Neal Maillet for making the idea for a book about hardy orchids a reality. Thanks, too, to Mindy Fitch, whose expert editing made this a much better book.

Native Orchid Conservation: One View

ANYONE SETTING OUT TO WRITE A BOOK ABOUT GROWING terrestrial orchids, especially North American native orchids, must necessarily prepare to meet an onslaught of criticism from people who believe encouraging gardeners to grow these plants will in turn encourage the removal of more plants from wild habitats. While granting that the ideal way to preserve biodiversity is to preserve intact natural habitats from incursion by development, it must be conceded that the consumption of land for a variety of purposes, from agriculture to parking lot construction, will continue to occur into the foreseeable future. As a matter of politics and policy, developers can count on working largely unfettered, in particular as converters of former agricultural land to homes and shopping centers. America's small agricultural enterprises fade from existence at such a rate that the word "vanishing" seems attached to the words "family farm" like a leech.

Often possessed of significant wooded areas, and always a patchwork of different kinds of habitat that could support a diversity of wild species, such lands daily fall victim to pavement and a seemingly unquenchable desire for a nice big house in the suburbs. All of this takes place in a climate of inadequate regulation, often zero public understanding or input, and always in the name of "progress," though our society seems woefully unable to define just what that means. To naysayers the pro-development camp issues stern reminders about "private property rights." Yet, what about the public good that comes from an undesecrated and fully functional ecosystem? Work must be done to help developers realize that some ecological resources actually increase in value when maintained rather than bulldozed. An urgent need exists to minimize the impact of the changes that will inevitably be wrought upon our native flora in every area of the United States, and, indeed, in most of North America during the twenty-first century.

Bringing wild species into cultivation and developing effective techniques for their large-scale propagation, something that humans have been doing with plants for tens of thousands of years, offers one helpful approach to maintaining wild populations of native plants and illuminating their ecology. As part of this effort, transplanting all or even a relatively small portion of threatened plant populations to protected sites in advance of the bulldozer offers several advantages. Transplantation preserves a sample of the gene pool. In addition, the plants become easily accessible to horticulturists and researchers, enabling cultivation and propagation techniques to develop in concert with scientific study. Not only can we learn to produce more individual plants, but as their needs become clear to us we also come to better understand their ecology. Furthermore, the most cost-effective way to accomplish this goal lies in having a thriving commercial industry in the species of interest. This should please my more conservative readers, who have by now no doubt envisioned acres of government-operated, taxpayer-funded greenhouses to produce rare native plants. I advocate nothing of the kind. Large-scale propagation and the preservation of samples of rare plant gene pools in both public and private gardens may offer the only route to avoiding extinction of numerous plant species—in particular those that possess narrowly defined ecological requirements, as is the case with orchids. But once those requirements are understood sufficiently to permit large-scale culture, the best way to produce the most plants at the least cost requires a business model, not another government boondoggle.

As a professional biologist, I have been occupied for most of my adult life with denizens of watery realms, from microscopic protozoans to sharks. Strange, then, that I would be writing a book about orchids, you may be thinking. On the contrary, hardy orchids are simply the current focus of my lifelong, passionate interest in nature. I spent a lot of time sloshing around in the streams and rivers of the southeastern United States, often in the company of experts, some of them the most brilliant minds in their respective disciplines. I struggled across slippery rocks in icy, rushing creeks in search of elusive, iridescent darters and venomous miniature catfishes. I floated lazily in the warm, shallow ocean off Grassy Key, Florida, observing a sea slug that appropriates the living photosynthetic chloroplasts from the seaweeds it eats, employing them as food as it basks in the warm tropical sun. During all that time, my colleagues and I were acutely aware of, and interested in, the myriad other life forms teeming around us. All of us had one or more ecology-related hobbies, apart from the specific objects of our scientific research. Mine happened to be orchids. Thus afforded many opportunities to learn ecology while standing, shivering, in a few feet of chilly water, listening to what my friends had to say about the catch of the moment, I eventually concluded that some basic principles of effective biodiversity management can be applied to any species or group, whether fish, fowl, or flower. To understand how these principles operate, we must begin by examining the land itself. Most of my experiences took place in the Tennessee Valley.

Although its rich bottomlands, vast stands of hardwood forest teeming with wildlife, and thousands of cool, crystal-clear streams abounding with fish have all been affected substantially by human encroachment, the Great Valley of the Tennessee River and the two ranges enclosing it remain relatively less developed than most of eastern North America. Consequently, they harbor a variety of species almost unparalleled within the temperate zone. To warm the valley's floor, the morning sun must ascend the majestic Blue Ridge, Unaka, and Great Smoky Mountains, collectively the crown jewels of the Appalachian chain extending from Maine to Georgia. Sheltered within those giant wrinkles in the earth's crust are more species of trees than in all of Europe. Whole families of amphibians continue to evolve here, and nowhere else, after millions of years. A substantial portion of the remaining virgin deciduous forest east of the Mississippi lies within this region, sometimes within the tens of thousands of acres designated the Cherokee National Forest.

The Great Valley itself consists of a series of parallel ridges alternating with narrow valleys running southwest to northeast, beginning at the foot of the mountains and extending roughly a hundred miles westward. Abundant rainfall flows down these ridges to gather in runs, branches, creeks, streams, brooks, and rivers almost too numerous to name. Undisturbed, any of these may harbor a dozen or more species of fish, with big rivers touting more than a hundred species. Before beavers were virtually exterminated in the early nineteenth century for their hides, which were used to make men's hats, they dammed any Great Valley stream of suitably low gradient, creating vast expanses of low-lying swamps edged with bogs. These swamps, along with the surrounding forest, probably nurtured an orchid flora that is now only patchily distributed within the region. Some of the rarest orchids grow in the remnants of the few natural bogs that remain. They can also be found growing in some artificial ones, the formation of which has been an unintended result of construction.

To the west of the Great Valley, the land abruptly rises, and the valley gives way to the Cumberland Plateau. Spared from many of the depredations of ax and bulldozer during the twentieth century, the Big South Fork National River and Recreation Area encompasses more than a million acres. Many ecologists believe the spectacular river gorge and the forest surrounding it may be even more biodiverse than the Great Smokies. Here, too, geology and climate have created a habitat abundantly colonized by orchids.

Having grown up in this region, I naturally took to the streams and creeks, even in my earliest childhood excursions. In the 1950s, even the smallest creeks harbored a few minnows. These I endlessly pursued with dip nets and mason jars. As elements of biodiversity, fish, in particular the ones living in the Great Valley, share many characteristics with native orchids. They may be extremely choosy about where they live. The Great Valley fish fauna includes species restricted in distribution, and quite a few rarities. So does the valley's orchid flora. What I have learned about finicky, unusual fish over the years can be applied analogously to orchids.

While the rest of the book concentrates on the horticulture of orchids found in the temperate zone, much of this chapter discusses threatened plants and at-risk ecosystems and what can be done to save them. Many of the orchid species discussed here are imperiled, often only because they characteristically live in places favored by humans for cities, farms, and factories. Thus, anyone who wishes to grow native orchids as a hobby or as part of a nursery business inevitably bumps up against various issues of conservation. Under what circumstances, if any, is the collection of wild plants acceptable? Can a system be developed that assures gardeners and nursery owners that plants have not been pillaged from public lands? Can propagation efforts produce enough plants to satisfy the market? I consider these issues important because conservationists have for years urged native plant enthusiasts to consider native orchids taboo as garden subjects. Why orchids have been singled out while others have not (gentians, for example) is an interesting question.

Part of the answer is that orchids have charisma. Small, rare species living in habitats that have been severely degraded or have drastically shrunk from preindustrialization size seldom enjoy the limelight. The same is true in the world of animals, where attention typically focuses upon species that are big, furry, or otherwise charming: whales, big cats, giant pandas, California condors, and spotted owls tend to steal the show. Such charismatic species clearly should be protected and allowed to repopulate their natural habitats; our planet would certainly be a less inspiring place were we to drive them to extinction. But focusing only upon a few obvious and entertaining aspects of a biosphere quite literally ignores the forest for the trees. When thinking about conservation, the general public often overlooks fish, marine invertebrates, insects, and native flowering plants. Alas, many of these are in greater danger of extinction than their more charismatic cousins, although they are seldom featured on CNN.

Native Orchids: Endangered Plants

While numerous orchids from Europe, South Africa, central Asia, and Australia can grow in North American gardens, with few exceptions the best performers are North American natives. When we consider growing native orchids, local wildflower conservation issues must necessarily be part of the discussion. Fortunately for our native plants, many individuals and organizations in America are dedicated to wildflower conservation. Sometimes, however, particularly in the case of native orchids, policies are adopted that are actually counterproductive. We can do a better job of protecting native orchids in the wild while still allowing people to enjoy them in home gardens.

Bill Farnham first contacted me in early May 2001. Knowing that I was operating a small mail-order nursery in my spare time, Bill thought I might be interested in purchasing the pink lady's slippers (*Cypripedium acaule*) he had just discovered. Tennessee law prohibits any nursery from purchasing more than ten plants of any endangered species in a calendar year, so a business deal was out. I was intrigued, however, with the knowledge that a stand of these beautiful orchids existed so close to Knoxville, less than a fifteen-minute drive from downtown.

On 13 May, camera in hand, I made the short trek into the woods with Bill. Less than a hundred yards from the main road, in a stand of pines with aromatic branches dappling the sunlight, the stately plants grew in profusion. Most were in full bloom. Based on Bill's description of the site, I'd expected a patch of about a hundred orchids. Prior excursions to observe and photograph pink lady's slippers had led me to believe that a clump of only two or three plants, or at most a modest group of a hundred or so, was typical. My first glimpse of this stand, however, literally caused a gasp to escape my lips. There were hundreds and hundreds of plants, growing in scattered groups as far as could be seen in any direction. What magnificent specimens many of them were. Some plants sported as many as seven or eight flower stems, indicating that they had been growing undisturbed for many years. This marvelous display, requiring perhaps fifty years or more to develop, would be gone in an instant when the bulldozers started rolling.

With Bill's permission, I returned several times to the site during spring and summer to study the orchids. A census of the plants indicated that there were at least five thousand individuals growing there, about a third of which were of blooming size. Using Global Positioning System (GPS) equipment, I determined that the majority were growing along a shallow swale bisecting the property from east to west.

Good fortune had provided this site with nearly optimal conditions for the growth of the pink lady's slippers: acid soil, good drainage, adequate moisture, and dappled sunlight. The pines, which were approximately fifty years old judging from the size of the largest ones, dominated the site, their fallen needles providing a layer of strongly acidic, well-drained compost about 4 inches deep atop the underlying yellow-orange clay. Only a few other types of plants grew alongside the lady's slippers. Mosses and a relative of wintergreen with the charming Native American name "pipsissewa" (*Chimaphila maculata*) were common. The site is more or less level, ensuring the ground remains

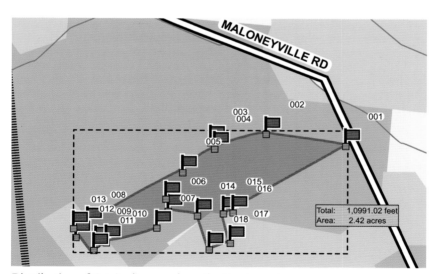

Distribution of *Cypripedium acaule* on the Farnham site.
GPS graphic by David Boruff and Paulo Reis.

19

damp but not saturated following a rain, thus creating moisture conditions ideal for pink lady's slippers.

During the summer I attempted to recruit the assistance of various groups and agencies in organizing a "rescue" of the plants. Since this species is on Tennessee's list of endangered plants, I e-mailed the state botanist's office at the Department of Environment and Conservation in Nashville. No reply was forthcoming. Nor did I hear anything from the botany department at the University of Tennessee. Gabby Call, director of protection for the Tennessee chapter of the Nature Conservancy, referred me to her husband, Geoff, a conservationist who works for the University of Tennessee Space Institute at Tullahoma. The Institute has a stand of pink lady's slippers on its property. I suggested the possibility of relocating some of Bill Farnham's plants there. Unfortunately, the institute rejected the idea, citing the species' poor record of successful transplantation, and concerns about introducing new genetic material from the eastern Tennessee population into the middle Tennessee population.

Late summer brought better luck. By coincidence, a local park's education director, Jackie Lane, attended the same church as Bill Farnham. Having just initiated a rare plant protection project, Jackie became interested in helping to rescue the lady's slippers after hearing about the plants in a conversation with Bill one Sunday morning. She recruited volunteers from among the region's numerous wildflower enthusiasts to participate in the dig.

On a perfect Sunday afternoon in October, about twenty of us gathered at the site with spades and plastic grocery bags. With this and two subsequent digs, one involving additional volunteers enlisted by Jackie and the other spearheaded by members of the Knoxville Association of Garden Clubs, we salvaged approximately eleven hundred plants. Some of these orchids became part of a permanent planting at Ijams Nature Center, others were sold to raise money for local conservation programs, and still others became the subjects of my research into better growing methods.

One of the most important things I learned about during my experience helping to rescue the pink lady's slippers was the inadequacy of

Cypripedium acaule blooms in my study bed the first spring after transplanting.

Cypripedium acaule research bed.

Tennessee's plant protection laws, which often appear to work counter to their intent. I fear this may be the case in other states as well. One problem in Tennessee arises because jurisdiction over wild plant conservation is split between two agencies, the Tennessee Department of Environment and Conservation (TDEC) and the Tennessee Department of Agriculture (TDA). The TDEC has jurisdiction over any plant placed on the state list of endangered species, which includes nearly 20 percent of the more than twenty-two hundred types of vascular plants native to Tennessee. As I've already mentioned, the Tennessee Rare Plant Protection Act of 1985, administered by the TDEC, restricts nurseries from purchasing more than ten plants of any state-listed endangered species in a calendar year. The law covers even nursery-propagated plants. Thus, no incentive exists for nurseries to propagate large numbers of rare plants. Yet the act clearly requires "that rare plants throughout this state be protected and conserved; that their numbers be maintained and enhanced; and that *propagative techniques be developed for them* to ensure their perpetuation" (emphasis added). The law thus treats the nursery trade, which adds millions of dollars each year to the state's economy, as if it were a threat to Tennessee's rare flora, despite the stated intent to develop propagative techniques.

According to former state botanist Carl Nordman, the pink lady's slipper was placed on the endangered species list because of a perception that the orchid was threatened by commercial digging. I was able to uncover no solid evidence upon which this perception might be based. In fact, according to the wildlife managers I corresponded with, individuals, not organizations, casually undertake most illegal digging of wild plants, presumably for transplantation to their private gardens. Lady's slippers are not, for example, offered in the catalogs of any of six retail wildflower nurseries in Tennessee and surrounding states, except for plants specifically described as the product of documented salvage efforts such as the one conducted on the Farnham site.

On the other hand, Tennessee wild plant dealers, "regulated" by the TDA, *legally* dig and sell thousands of wild plants each year. Anyone who fills out an application and pays a $100 fee can become a wild plant dealer. The TDA recommends, but does not require, permission

of the landowner be obtained before collecting plants. Wild plant dealers are exempt from the ten-plant limit imposed on nursery owners and
may have any number of unlicensed collectors working for them. No li-
cense is needed to collect wild plants, only to sell them.

Private landowners are under no special obligation with respect to
the plants, endangered or not, growing on their property. The Rare
Plant Protection Act specifies that "nothing [in this act] shall be con-
strued to limit the rights of private property owners to take rare plants
from their own lands or to manage their lands for agriculture, forestry,
development or any other lawful purpose." Since roughly 92 percent of
Tennessee's land area is private property, the fate of Tennessee's vanishing flora is by and large in the hands of individuals. Let's hope the
majority of them are at least as conscientious as Bill Farnham.

A common misconception regarding the orchid flora of North America
is that most, if not all, species are protected by the Endangered Species
Act. In fact, thankfully, only seven of the native orchids found in the
forty-eight contiguous states are on the list of endangered and threatened plant species maintained by the federal government. Additional
plants, however, may be considered "endangered, threatened or of special concern" within a single state by agencies charged with environmental protection in that state.

Worldwide regulation of trade in all orchid species falls under the
Convention on International Trade in Endangered Species (CITES).
Shipment of orchids across international boundaries requires permits.
Hardy orchids imported into the United States from other countries
must be accompanied by paperwork from the exporting country at-
testing that various requirements have been met. Orchid importers,
likewise, require permits issued by the government. By monitoring the
trade and compiling enough statistics, it is theoretically possible to identify potential overexploitation of wild plants in time to take corrective
action.

Worldwide, orchid populations dwindle largely due to encroachment upon their habitats by human activities. In the United States,
whose rate of real estate development surpasses that of any other coun-

try, native orchids have already disappeared from many sites and are declining in others, mostly because they cannot compete for the land. Orchids may occupy low-lying areas near the margins of lakes or along rivers and streams. Some of the most horticulturally desirable species live in bogs. Humans have founded towns along the banks of rivers for centuries and have drained countless acres of bogs to render sites more amenable to construction and agriculture. Such actions have drastically reduced the number of places orchids are able to colonize. The pace of land consumption staggers the senses. Each year in Tennessee a county-size swatch of the landscape disappears under asphalt and concrete. In 1999 the rate of conversion of land to development in Tennessee was the fifth highest in the nation. Native plant habitat vanishes daily.

While we should continue setting aside new public lands for the preservation of the flora and fauna inhabiting them, the rate of wild land protection lags significantly behind the rate of conversion to development. Common sense suggests that land development will continue for the foreseeable future. Literally millions of native plants could be rescued from development sites. With landowner permission and appropriate licenses and permits from state or federal agencies, horticulturists and others interested in wild plants should be allowed to carry out salvage digging for purposes of study, propagation, or even immediate sale to the nursery industry. Garden clubs and conservation groups infrequently arrange salvage digs to remove plants from areas awaiting the imminent arrival of a bulldozer. Plants obtained in this manner might be donated to botanical gardens, relocated to protected lands, or sold to raise money for the group doing the digging. Salvage digging is currently the only way that some orchid species can be made available to the grower. Eventually, however, it will be possible to produce all the horticulturally desirable hardy orchids via propagation techniques now in use for other orchid species. Developing such techniques will require that some wild plants be made available for cultivation attempts and long-term study.

Growing plants in artificial habitats is one way to ensure that orchid species will always be around to enjoy. Large numbers of gardeners scattered across the country create an enormous reservoir of plant genetic material by growing regionally adapted strains of their local wildflowers. Should not orchids, some of the most intriguing and attractive species, be included in these efforts? Further, as gardeners explore and develop their interests in uncommon plants such as orchids, their appreciation of the need to conserve and protect wild plant populations increases. Orchids possess enough personality to attract widespread attention. Preserving orchid habitats simultaneously protects an entire ecosystem, including symbiotic fungi, pollinators, and all the other species, such as mites and mosses, that might not, at least to most people, share the beauty and charm of an orchid.

Wildflower field guides and gardening books often strongly discourage *any* taking of wild plants for horticultural purposes. For example, with regard to the North American *Cypripedium* species, or lady's slippers, Jones and Foote (1990) wrote, "Since they are difficult to establish, they are not recommended for the average gardener. Lady's Slippers purchased from nurseries represent collected material as commercial propagation is not yet feasible. Commercial digging of plants from the wild is a deplorable practice." When the book was written, it was true that no commercial sources for propagated lady's slippers were yet in existence. Since that time, however, several companies have sprung up to propagate not only lady's slippers but also various other hardy orchids (see "Suppliers and Organizations"). Nevertheless, in 1998 the noted garden writer Jack Kramer, in *Botanical Orchids and How to Grow Them*, said of cypripediums: "These terrestrial orchids do not transplant well, and they are not easy to grow if you buy them from a supplier. Cyps are an endangered species and so should never be gathered in the wild." Only the rare *Cypripedium kentuckiense* is considered federally endangered, and Kramer makes no mention of cultivated sources for these plants, although when the book came out, nurseries offered propagated specimens.

It seems a shame that plants are destroyed by the thousands to build shopping malls, factories, schools, and parking lots, particularly when there are hundreds of eager gardeners waiting to give them new homes. Garden writers too often fail to credit their readers with the good sense to seek out ecologically viable sources of native orchids. The list of suppliers and organizations included at the back of this book, for example, provides an excellent place to begin. Pricing can often be a guide to the provenance of the plants, as legally dug or greenhouse-propagated specimens typically sell for prices similar to those charged for tropical orchids at the same stage of growth. In other words, for blooming-size plants, expect to pay $20 or more, with an additional premium for a rare or difficult-to-propagate species. Plants obtained under questionable circumstances are typically much cheaper, sometimes offered for only a dollar or two. Resist the temptation to purchase them, and inquire closely regarding the source. Speak your mind to the dealer about the damage unauthorized collecting does, to the ecosystem as well as to the public image of the horticultural industry and, indeed, to the reputations of native plant enthusiasts.

If you cannot obtain a species through legal, sustainable means, or if you do not possess the knowledge or resources to cultivate it successfully, you should be content to enjoy observing it in the wild. However, the most horticulturally desirable native and hardy exotic orchid species are already being propagated, and your patronage of the nurseries that grow them will ensure that larger numbers of choice clones will be cultivated in the future. Developing horticultural methods for native orchids provides increased potential for rescue by relocation of wild stands threatened by development, and makes recovery and restoration planting on reclaimed or protected sites more feasible.

Some garden writers appear to hold the view that encouraging hobby gardeners to pursue an interest in growing hardy orchids will result in an increase in irresponsible removal of wild plants. However, recent successes in laboratory propagation, the development of "documented plant salvage" programs, and a growing fund of cultural information all make enjoying these plants at home without threatening them in the wild an achievable goal. Even so, garden literature abounds with misinformation concerning both the horticulture and conservation of native orchids. For example, some imply commercial digging is a major threat to all species of wildflowers in North America. Available evidence indicates that advancing development is a far greater problem. I admire these authors for their contributions to plant conservation, but I must respectfully disagree with the idea that transplanting wild plants to the garden is always wrong.

The best way to protect native plants is to protect the habitats where they occur. This is known as *in situ* conservation. National and state parks, together with reserves owned by groups such as the Nature Conservancy, protect species *in situ* by preventing development of their habitats.

My experience as an ichthyologist taught me the importance of another tool for preserving biodiversity. Known as *ex situ* conservation, this method preserves species by propagating them away from their native habitats. Growing native plants in private gardens and nurseries constitutes *ex situ* conservation.

Are the species that draw the greatest interest from native plant gardeners also those threatened with extinction? Brumbeck (1988) and Campbell (1988) found that of six hundred species of native plants offered for sale in mail-order catalogs, only one appeared on the federal list of endangered and threatened species. A few federally listed plants, such as the Tennessee coneflower (*Echinacea tennesseensis*), are currently offered in garden catalogs, but in all cases the plants are advertised as nursery propagated. Wildflower enthusiasts should understand that trilliums and orchids are not the major interests of plant diggers. Ginseng (*Panax quinquefolius*), valued by some for its reputed medicinal and aphrodisiac properties, is so extensively dug in Tennessee that it is regulated separately from other plants. Goldenseal (*Hydrastis canadensis*) languishes on the edge of decimation because of its perceived value to herbalists. The dubious distinction of being the most commonly dug wild plant, though, belongs to eastern hemlock (*Tsuga canadensis*). One of our most desirable and widely grown landscape evergreens, eastern hemlock germinates poorly and resists rooting from cuttings. Consequently, wild seedlings grown out in a nursery constitute the supply of these trees, including the potted hemlocks at your local big-box retailer.

Campbell (1988) concluded that "over 100,000 herbaceous plants are removed annually from the woodlands of North Carolina and Tennessee." Is this level of digging wreaking devastation in the woods? For purposes of illustration, assume that all of these plants were taken from an area the size of the Great Smoky Mountains National Park, which encompasses 540,000 acres. The annual harvest would amount to only 5.4 plants per acre. Even if the rate of digging has quadrupled in the intervening years, that would still be only 25 plants per acre. On the other hand, deforestation and the conversion of undeveloped or agricultural land to commercial or industrial development in Tennessee consumed some 122,000 acres annually between 1992 and 1997, according to the U.S. Department of Agriculture (USDA) Natural Resources Conservation Service (1999). Thus, in a mere five years an area roughly 20 percent larger than the Great Smoky Mountains National Park was destroyed. In North Carolina the conversion rate was even more rapacious, gobbling up more than 156,000 acres per year. Conversion to development means *all* native plants on the site are lost, to be replaced with asphalt, buildings, or landscaping often comprised entirely of non-native species. People who consider it a travesty that a few wild plants dug from a roadside ditch may find their way into the hands of gardeners, yet who keep silent about the millions of similar plants killed by bulldozers and herbicides each year in the name of progress, are, in my humble opinion, missing the point entirely.

Home gardeners may sometimes have an unanticipated role to play in preserving native plant species. In Great Britain the population of the European yellow lady's slipper (*Cypripedium calceolus*) dwindled to just one wild plant. With the help of seeds and pollen provided by British gardeners, the species has a chance to survive (Cribb 1997).

Environmentally conscious gardeners, which includes the vast majority of us, do not condone illegal or casual digging of wild plants, especially on public lands. The unauthorized removal of wild plants is not only ethically wrong but in many instances illegal. Special permits are required to remove plants from public lands, and permission is typically granted only for scientific research. Removal of plants from private lands without the landowner's permission constitutes theft.

Often, land intended for timber production is the source of wild-dug plants. Clear-cutting, which routinely takes place on private land

Cypripedium calceolus. Photo by W. George Schmid.

and increasingly in public forests, not only destroys the entire forest ecosystem but also disrupts natural migration patterns, increases deleterious "edge effects" in adjacent ecosystems, and contributes to water quality problems. As long as the U.S. Forest Service allows the timber industry to remove the trees, why not allow the nursery industry to remove the horticulturally desirable plants as well?

Local awareness and involvement, thoughtful government policy based on scientific research, and consideration of the entire ecosystem, not just its components, in policymaking and planning characterize the most sound approach to wild plant conservation, an approach that can work anywhere. If acted upon, the following suggestions would vastly improve the odds of long-term survival for North American native plant species and the ecosystems they support:

1. Create more public parks and reserves owned and maintained by local communities.
2. Eliminate most logging and mining on public lands.
3. Engineer programs to relocate plants from areas slated for logging, road construction, or other development to areas under protection.
4. Require public works projects to include in environmental assessments the composition of impacted plant communities, with a view toward on-site preservation, or failing that, salvage.
5. Create a certification system, administered by states but with uniform federal guidelines, independent of the nursery industry, to distinguish salvaged and propagated native plants in the nursery trade, permitting consumers to make informed choices.
6. Support public and private botanical gardens, encouraging not only the expansion in acreage of existing gardens where feasible but also an increase in the number of individual institutions, so that many more localities will lie within a short drive of one.

7. Require plantings of native species in public works landscaping, such as along roadsides.
8. Establish native plant gene banks, based on species and population assessments at the county level.
9. Compile and maintain an integrated database of plant species held in botanical garden and conservatory collections.
10. Encourage programs, such as that of the North American Plant Preservation Council, to maintain a database of plant species in the collections of private gardeners.
11. Include information about native plant gardening and *ex situ* conservation in school curricula.
12. Offer tax credits at the local, state, and federal levels to individuals who preserve, propagate, or restore certain species on their own property.

Medicinal Properties of Hardy Orchids

Should the mere existence of things so beautiful and captivating as native orchids provide insufficient encouragement for their preservation and propagation, consider their potential value as sources of new medicines. Ever since first reading about the sedative effects of cypripedium rhizomes (Cribb 1997), I have speculated on the possibility that nearly all hardy terrestrial orchids, because they undergo winter dormancy, may contain in their fleshy underground parts an array of bioactive compounds that should be carefully investigated for their pharmacological properties. Considered in light of the various species' ecological needs and annual growth cycles, endowing the orchids with an arsenal of phytochemicals makes good evolutionary sense.

Each hardy orchid plant invests a large portion of its resources in developing its swollen roots, tuberoid, or rhizome (as the varied forms are called). This structure provides a food reserve for next season's growth bud. It also functions as insurance against any catastrophe that might befall the aboveground portion of the plant during the growing season. The depredations of insects or animals might not only prevent flowering but could also, by defoliation, dramatically shorten the effective growing season and reduce the time available for accumulating food reserves. Without stored food, next year's growth might not be possible. With it, the orchid has another opportunity to escape disaster and, more importantly, to produce its thousands of seeds. The orchid therefore greatly increases it chances for long-term survival and successful reproduction by devising an effective hedge against bad times. Many other plants do the same thing. Phytochemicals can be exquisitely fine-tuned for specific functions. Certain species of *Ophrys*, for example, mimic not only the appearance but also the pheromones of female insects. Male insects pollinate the orchids while attempting to copulate with pseudofemales. Alkaloids in some members of the legume, hop, poppy, jimsonweed, and tomato families, just to name a few, can exert effects in humans ranging from euphoria to hallucinations to agonizing death. Small wonder if it turns out that most terrestrial orchid rootstocks also contain chemical deterrents to predation. Phytochemicals remain the primary source material for new medicines. Hardy orchids may be far more valuable than we even imagine. After confirming their potential value to medicine, we shall certainly need to know how to grow them.

Field Notes, 29 November 2003

Visited Farnham site. Temperature = 42°F. Site preparation for construction is beginning. Already many trees are down, and they are demolishing the old house, barn, and sheds. A bulldozer parked on the site looks like a sleeping monster. Deep, muddy ruts block my usual access point. Exposed everywhere, the bare ground holds water from the recent heavy rains, and all the plants and trees have been uprooted at the edge of the clearing. Deeper into the grove of pines, everything looks the same as before, with the exception of the fluorescent orange survey stakes and markers everywhere. Their arrangement suggests nothing, although I assume they are contour lines for the grading. Running cedar (*Lycopodium*) carpets the ground in big swaths, bright green after the rain, glistening with moisture from the recently departed morning frost. Dark green pipsissewa, emerald hair cap moss, and ghostly gray reindeer moss, interspersed with the lately fallen pine nee-

Cypripedium acaule blooms along a fallen log at the Farnham site.

dles, spread over the moist ground in patches, as if quilts were distributed under the pines in preparation for a picnic. Using GPS, I return to a large stand of orchids growing at the base of a fallen tree. I can see the empty seed capsules held aloft from the fallen leaves like periscopes. By spring, everything here will be gone, and a subdivision will be under construction. I return home, dig into the mulch under the white pine tree, and reassure myself that the lady's slippers rescued from this site are still doing well. The fuzzy, pale green growth points lie just beneath the surface, awaiting the arrival of spring and another opportunity to attract a bumblebee.

General Principles
of Hardy Orchid
Cultivation

ORCHIDS OCCUR IN EVERY STATE. FIFTY SPECIES ARE found in my home state of Tennessee, according to records in the University of Tennessee Herbarium. The herbarium lists no fewer than fourteen orchids from the densely populated Knox County alone, including *Aplectrum hyemale, Calopogon tuberosus, Corallorhiza odontorhiza, C. wisteriana, Cypripedium acaule, C. pubescens, Galearis spectabilis, Goodyera pubescens, Hexalectris spicata, Liparis liliifolia, Platanthera ciliaris, Spiranthes cernua* var. *odorata, S. lacera* var. *gracilis,* and *Tipularia discolor*. Although not all regions of the country are this kindly favored botanically, orchids live everywhere except the driest deserts and permanently frozen arctic regions. There are almost certainly native orchids where you live.

Part of the reason I first became interested in growing native orchids stemmed directly from their reputation for fussiness in cultivation. In no reference book could I find any encouragement for including native orchids in my wildflower garden; in fact, most of the books I consulted contained numerous exhortations to avoid even attempting to grow them. Eventually, after tramping along miles of woodland trails in search of orchids to photograph, I decided these books must be wrong. I observed that orchids frequently turn up in marginal or recently disturbed habitats and often colonize areas that are inimical to many other types of plants. European bee orchids (*Ophrys* species) often colonize construction sites and roadsides (Cribb and Bailes 1989). One of the better sites I know for observing *Platanthera* orchids lies underneath a high-voltage power line tower. The ability of orchids to grow in locations in which other plants cannot often shields the orchids from competition. Absence of competition, in fact, appears to be the primary requirement for many orchid species in the wild. In the Great Smoky Mountains National Park, native orchids often occur in large stands unsullied by a commingling of other wildflowers.

Similarly, only a few well-adapted species occupy the *Cypripedium acaule* site described in chapter 1. Besides the orchids, the most numerous species are lichens, mosses, and ferns, along with the Virginia pine trees responsible for the special characteristics of the habitat. Very few flowering plants, and only those adapted to acidic, nutrient-poor soils, are present. Exotics, unfortunately, have begun to claim the site. Poison ivy and Japanese honeysuckle have encroached noticeably from their founding populations at the perimeter of the woods, even in the few seasons during which I have been visiting. Southern pine borers fell a few trees each year, opening up new space to full sun. In such places the orchids would be expected to enjoy several seasons of luxuriant growth and flowering before being overrun by the ivy and honeysuckle. In a few years these weeds will dominate the site, should its planned development not take place. I suspect boggy sites occupied by native orchids face similar danger from the rapacious purple loosestrife in the Midwest and Northeast.

Given the proclivities of hardy orchids toward extreme habitats, they should be a cinch to grow. After all, other plants capable of colonizing barren sites literally grow like weeds in the garden. Most of them, in fact, *are* weeds. Why not orchids?

It turns out that although orchids have successful strategies for dealing with extreme habitats, they lack adaptability. Only habitats that fulfill a specific set of growth requirements will support orchids. Roadside weeds, on the other hand, readily grow on a variety of soils and under an array of sunshine and water regimens. This consideration overrides all others in developing strategies for growing hardy orchids. Fortunately, comparatively few combinations of culture conditions work well for all the species of horticultural interest. A bog habitat with areas of full sun, dappled shade, and shade will accommodate the largest number of hardy orchids. A barren pile of pine bark chips and sand in partial sun will accommodate others. A small minority can be grown successfully alongside more familiar shade plants, like hostas.

With regard to the pH of the growing medium, discussed later in this chapter, hardy orchids tend to cluster into four groups, with some overlap. For example:

GROUP 1
pH 3.5–5
  Platanthera blephariglottis
pH 4–5
  Cypripedium acaule
  Platanthera cristata
  Platanthera integra
  Pogonia ophioglossoides
  Spiranthes cernua
pH 4–5.5
  Malaxis unifolia
pH 4–6
  Calopogon tuberosus

GROUP 2
pH 4.5–5
  Platanthera clavellata
  Platanthera flava
pH 4.5–5.5
  Arethusa bulbosa
pH 4.5–6
  Pyrola uniflora
pH 4.5–6.5
  Liparis loeselii

GROUP 3
pH 5–6
  Corallorhiza maculata
  Cypripedium arietinum
  Cypripedium parviflorum
  Epipactis helleborine
  Goodyera pubescens
  Isotria verticillata
  Liparis liliifolia
  Listera cordata
  Platanthera lacera
  Platanthera nivea
  Platanthera peramoena
  Platanthera psycodes
  Spiranthes lacera
  Spiranthes vernalis
  Tipularia discolor
pH 5–6.5
  Platanthera orbiculata
pH 5.5–6.5
  Corallorhiza wisteriana
pH 5.5–7
  Triphora trianthophora

GROUP 4

pH 6–7
  Calypso bulbosa
  Corallorhiza odontorhiza
  Corallorhiza trifida
  Cypripedium calceolus
  Galearis spectabilis
pH 6–8
  Cypripedium reginae
  Platanthera repens

pH 6.5–7
  Hexalectris spicata
pH 7–8
  Cypripedium montanum
  Spiranthes lucida

Such a level of habitat specificity actually makes the gardener's task far simpler. Why then have so many found these plants difficult to grow? Most of the problem, I suspect, lies in trying to grow them alongside other plants. Most of the wildflower gardens I have seen are much more like botanical display cases than the native woods or fields they are supposed to represent. Indeed, my own garden falls into the display case category. In Frozen Head State Park near my home, yellow lady's slippers grow along the same trail only a few feet away from stands of *Trillium grandiflorum*, *Disporum maculatum*, and *Uvularia grandiflora*. In the garden, however, the orchid will not succeed in the soils in which these other genera thrive. It requires a growing medium tailored to its needs; interestingly, the other plants will grow in that medium, too, but the orchid will not grow in the variety of media that support the other plants.

Another reason for failure with orchids in the garden has to do with watering technique, whether providing too much water or watering at the wrong time. Natural rainfall should be sufficient for orchids native to an area if they are growing in beds sunk into the ground. (Raised beds often require some irrigation because they dry out readily.) Applying extra water during the orchid's dormant period or when the temperature remains too low for vigorous growth often leads to problems.

Finally, pH and its relation to the availability of nutrients in the growing medium must be given consideration. Orchids that naturally live in strongly acidic soils, for example, may be killed by overfertilization, while plants normally accustomed to neutral conditions may yellow and fail to bloom unless fed.

The key to hardy orchid cultivation lies in understanding the habitat-specific adaptations of the plants. Members of the orchid family share some of these adaptations. Consequently, gardeners experienced with tropical orchids will readily note the parallels in culture technique. Species-specific adaptations, such as a demand for low pH, or the interestingly reversed growing season, or summer dormancy, of species like *Ophrys* and *Tipularia*, do apply to some hardy orchids. However, these special needs may be dealt with easily.

Nearly all hardy orchids are terrestrial, meaning they grow in the ground, as do most flowering plants. In fact, the majority of orchid species are terrestrial. The tropical orchids favored by enthusiasts, by contrast, are mostly epiphytic, growing in the crook of a tree limb or on a moss-covered branch. Tropical orchids certainly hold the lion's share of interest for the indoor gardener, but the terrestrials have more to offer the outdoor gardener, blooming either with long-time favorites such as tulips or at odd times when little else is in bloom. Fragrance, brilliant color display, and longevity also recommend hardy orchids as horticultural subjects.

Unique Features of the Orchid Family

Orchids possess some interesting deviations from the norm for flowering plants. Coincidentally, their genetic predilections also encourage orchids to succeed in trying circumstances. Why do native orchids have a reputation for being difficult to cultivate, when tropical orchids have been cultivated successfully for decades?

Plant anatomy often determines culture requirements. For example, because the roots of tropical orchids are susceptible to rot if kept too moist, they require a sharply drained growing medium. Might this not also be the case with hardy orchids? One quickly learns that it is.

Many of the hardy orchids in which a gardener might be interested grow naturally in bogs. A bog is not a pond filled with moss. The sphagnum moss that dominates true bog habitats acts as a conduit for the slow diffusion of water from the underlying aquifer to the surface, allowing oxygen to reach the roots of the plants growing in the moss carpet. If the bog held water like a pond, the plant roots would be thrust into an oxygen-depleted environment and would be quickly replaced by species that can grow with their roots submerged, such as cattails. Draining the bog, on the other hand, leaves too little moisture behind, and plants such as ironweed, milkweed, and showy goldenrod appear, eventually to be followed by tree seedlings. Thus, merely mimicking the moisture conditions of the bog habitat in a garden bed enables gardeners to grow and flower a wide range of orchid species. Attempting to locate the orchids alongside other native plants, such as phlox or trilliums, in a typical woodland soil generally leads to failure, as does planting more rampantly growing moisture lovers, such as cattails, alongside the orchids.

I suspect many a frustrated novice simply fails to take into account that any given geographic area, even one as small as a building lot, may consist of a patchwork of microhabitats, each characterized by variations in parameters such as the amount of sun or shade, the moisture retentiveness of the soil or lack thereof, exposure to wind, and the presence or absence of competing species. Anyone doubting this need only compare the vegetation growing along the interstate ramp near my house with the vegetation growing in the swale 30 feet away. In late summer the dry-baked area of clay soil along the asphalt blooms with *Rudbeckia*, *Bidens*, and *Coreopsis*, while the low-lying area beyond boasts stands of *Typha* and *Sagittaria*. Among these vigorously invasive moisture lovers, the dusty-rose-colored plumes of *Eupatorium maculatum* and the scarlet spires of *Lobelia cardinalis* call out to swarms of butterflies. Even the grasses differ between the two locations. Three or four years ago the area was stripped down to the clay subsoil, compacted by the movements of construction equipment, and changed utterly from its former status as a cow pasture. Yet, seeds have blown in from undisturbed areas nearby, the activities of birds, small mammals, and humans have brought in still more, and once again the land blooms. Tree seedlings are already showing up, sorted according to their moisture preferences, just like the herbaceous plants. Nature's hallmark is this kind of resilience and exuberance.

Why then aren't the roadsides teeming with orchids? Actually, in some areas they are, when conditions favor them, although this is certainly not a commonplace occurrence. Orchids at least *seem* relatively rare. While some orchids are indeed extremely rare, they can be amazingly abundant in the right spot. This observation reinforces our strategy for developing successful culture methods: identify the parameters that appear to favor orchids in the wild, and then attempt to mimic these conditions at home.

MOISTURE CONTENT OF THE GROWING MEDIUM

Typically, hardy orchids require a relatively constant level of soil moisture during the growing season. This may be naturally maintained in any of several ways. In the most common situation, the water table lies close to the surface, perhaps within a foot or less, and moisture permeates a loose, fluffy compost made up of plant debris and often mosses. Evaporation from the surface causes water to diffuse upward from the water table through the compost, but the compost itself never becomes waterlogged. Such conditions are typical of bogs. True bog habitat is now rare in the southern Appalachians, but in more northerly regions of the country, bogs are common and are often home to an abundant orchid flora.

In the southeastern mountains, a similar habitat for orchids often develops at the edge of a creek or stream, especially where the grade approaches level, and water easily percolates into the underlying substrate. This can even occur where a roadside drainage ditch is flanked by a layer of construction aggregate. At points along the Roaring Fork Motor Nature Trail in the Great Smoky Mountains National Park, the roadbed is only a few inches higher than the surface of its namesake stream, winding 10–25 feet from the road, down the narrow valley between Mount Winnesoka and Piney Mountain. Roaring Fork tumbles precipitously from near the summit of Mount LeConte, dropping in elevation nearly 2000 feet within its first 2 miles. On the valley floor the slope is far more gentle, and Roaring Fork becomes broader and correspondingly gentler. The motor trail alongside Roaring Fork consists of a layer of asphalt atop about 4 inches of crushed limestone. The limestone forms a broad shoulder along the roadside in places where it has been pushed away from the asphalt and scattered toward the creek by the pressure of the thousands of cars and RVs that circle the trail each year. A constant rain of plant matter falls from the forest canopy or is carried by Roaring Fork during floods to form a compost that fills the spaces in the limestone gravel layer. Such places are home to an abundance of showy orchids (*Galearis spectabilis*), an otherwise uncommon species. Road construction within forested areas appears to favor showy orchids, which may benefit not only from the extra lime in their growing medium but also from increased sun exposure at the road's edge. I have often observed this species within a few feet of a parking area or mountain road. Nevertheless, this observation should not be taken to suggest we need more road construction through our southeastern forests!

Another specialized moisture condition occurs in the areas favored by orchids that prefer a strongly acidic growing medium. Poor, impermeable clay subsoils form where silt once accumulated in low-lying, relatively flat areas, such as on the floor of the Tennessee Valley. Lying undisturbed by humans for millennia, these areas were cloaked in magnificent deciduous and mixed forests until relatively modern times. Unfortunately for the flora, level areas near water were among the most desirable locations for pioneering humans, and most of the original forest cover was quickly cut to make room for farms and towns. When the land was exhausted from agriculture, or further denuded by a second round of clear-cutting in the early twentieth century, it was often abandoned. Such sites are now frequently dominated by stands of fifty-to hundred-year-old pine trees. As a layer of pine needles accumulates on the surface of the clay, a growing medium for orchids (and certain other plants characteristic of this habitat type) slowly develops. Each time the region's abundant rainfall arrives, it quickly penetrates the layer of pine duff, but is held in place temporarily by the layer of clay, like coffee spilled on a flat tabletop. Before the water completely drains away, it can be carried up through the duff by capillary action. In this manner a relatively constant low level of moisture is maintained around the roots of the orchids growing in the layer of well-aerated organic matter.

Only one of the orchids mentioned in this book, *Spiranthes cernua*, grows well with submerged roots, a capability that has led to it being called the "aquatic orchid" in water-gardening circles. Nevertheless, this orchid grows and flowers quite well in the same bog garden conditions favored by *Cypripedium* and *Platanthera*.

From these examples it can be seen that most hardy orchids do best in a loose, fluffy, organic growing medium capable of holding moisture without becoming waterlogged; fine-textured media such as the peat-based potting mixes used for many indoor and outdoor plants smother the roots of hardy orchids and rapidly kill them. Orchidists often exhort us to use a growing mix that "retains moisture but is nevertheless well drained," or words to that effect, but what exactly is a well-drained growing medium?

In an attempt to resolve the question, I decided to compare a mix that works for *Cypripedium acaule*, a particularly finicky orchid, with media composed of other commonly used materials. I mixed up a fresh batch of four media: a basic woodland wildflower mix, tropical orchid bark, a bog orchid mix, and a *C. acaule* mix that includes PermaTill, a mineral product equivalent to very coarse sand.

I used these media to fill standard 6-inch plastic pots, as if repotting a plant, and left them sitting in the sun all day to dry out. I then poured 2 liters of water into each pot, allowed the pots to drain into plastic tubs for fifteen minutes, and measured the amount of water in the tubs. Subtracting this from 2 liters gave the amount of water retained by each medium: 560 ml for the woodland wildflower mix, 250 ml for the tropical orchid bark, 300 ml for the bog orchid mix, and 155 ml for the *Cypripedium acaule* mix.

Tropical orchid bark would have garnered my bet for minimal water retention, but the *Cypripedium acaule* mix proved to dry out most quickly, probably owing to the absorbency of the bark versus the complete nonabsorbency of the PermaTill. Based on this simple experiment, I propose we regard a mix that retains about 10 percent of the volume of water applied as well drained but moisture retentive.

SUN EXPOSURE

Any tropical orchid enthusiast who has ever allowed a prized plant to get a sunburn understands another critical factor for hardy orchid cultivation: providing the correct amount of sun exposure. In the Sunbelt, where summer temperatures may reach 100°F, an orchid that is located in too much sun will cook, literally, in one afternoon. Through painful experience I have learned to err on the side of too much shade. If the plant does not bloom after a year or two but otherwise grows well, perhaps it needs more sun, but wait until you have good reason before relocating it. For a mixed planting of hardy orchids, dappled shade such as that provided by high deciduous tree branches gives the best results. If the plants receive any direct sun, morning sun is best, while afternoon sun is less preferable. Avoid midday sun, which is the most intense. Tropical orchid enthusiasts will note that this is also true for the species they grow. Trees with spreading branches near the ground—dogwoods, for example—may provide excellent cover for shade-loving species, such as some platantheras. For species that need a bit more sun, such as cypripediums, some lower limbs may need to be pruned to open up the growing area to more light. Pruning should be done carefully and conservatively, as lopping off the wrong branch may be a mistake impossible to correct.

Altering the sun exposure may be difficult to accomplish in an outdoor garden. Properly siting the hardy orchid bed or beds right from the start will prevent you from having to relocate them later, or resorting to other costly or time-consuming measures such as pruning or planting additional shade trees. You may thus find it helpful to grow the orchid plants in pots for the first year or two. Place the pots where you want the plants eventually to reside, and see how they fare. This approach provides a "dress rehearsal," allowing you to evaluate the design of the bed and permitting a quick rearrangement if mistakes have been made. Inevitably, of course, mistakes will be made. Therefore, I recommend this method for any rare or valuable plant in your collection, even though you may be an experienced gardener.

Not long ago I moved to a new house on the other side of town, which involved relocating my entire plant collection of twenty-five years. As anyone who has ever moved will understand, many decisions about accommodating the new plants were arrived at on the spur of the moment. That fall, much transplanting needed to be accomplished, mostly to give each species its proper sun exposure. Orchids are inherently tough, however, and only two plants out of more than two hundred suffered from the move.

Artificial shade, in the form of a lath house, pergola, or similar structure, may be one alternative if the otherwise perfect spot for hardy orchids receives too much sun. The most shading will be needed on the south side of the bed, but do not make the mistake, as I once did, of failing to take into account the potential effects of exposure when the sun's rays arrive at a low angle, early or late in the day. I have damaged *Cypripedium* plants by neglecting to shade them from the western sun. The fail-safe approach to designing artificial shade for hardy orchids is to enclose the growing area completely. A screened porch or deck with a lath roof shade will provide the dappled, constantly shifting patterns of light the plants seem to prefer. When considering this approach, remember that the design and construction of the shade structure must always conform to local building codes. Overhead shade structures in particular must be well made and properly installed to avoid any possibility that they might come crashing down on you or your guests. Always seek professional advice if you have any doubts about the design.

Half-hardy terrestrial orchids are those able to tolerate a minimum temperature of about 40°F. Even in my zone 7 garden, sheltered spots can nurture plants that otherwise would not survive the average winter low. A frost-free but cold greenhouse or "alpine house" offers the best protection for a collection of half-hardy plants, and becomes essential as you move north out of the southeastern and southwestern corners of the country. Many native orchids of Europe, the Middle East, Asia, and Australia belong to the half-hardy group.

HUMIDITY

Another unique anatomical feature of the orchid family is the absence of guard cells around the tiny leaf openings, or stomata, that allow the leaves to "breathe." In most plants the guard cells can shrink or swell depending upon the plant's water needs of the moment. Not so with orchids, which therefore are at the mercy of their environment. Hardy orchids, like their tropical cousins, thrive best when the relative humidity is above 40 percent. For the outdoor gardener, maintaining this level of humidity may not be a big concern, especially if you are growing plants native to your area. Humidity does become a factor with plants growing in containers. Increased air circulation around container plants makes them liable to damage if the growing medium dries out. During warm weather, plants in containers may need to be checked daily for the correct moisture level. Orchids, unfortunately, do not really wilt to warn of imminent water damage as many familiar garden plants do. A water shortage usually appears as damage to the leaf tips, damage that will remain unrepaired until the orchid loses that leaf.

pH OF THE GROWING MEDIUM
In the wild, orchids often colonize marginal habitats. On one site with which I am familiar, the strongly acidic soil formed underneath pines and other conifers favors *Cypripedium acaule*, *Goodyera pubescens*, *Tipularia discolor*, and *Platanthera ciliaris*. Few other native plants have succeeded on this site. *Chimaphila maculata* and *Lonicera sempervirens* are two of the more notable ones. Pest plants such as poison ivy and Japanese honeysuckle grow on the site where enough sun filters through the pines. Otherwise, not much goes on here botanically. Multiple orchid species are often found growing together or with certain companion plants. Bentley (2000) mentions the regularity with which *Cypripedium acaule* and *Goodyera pubescens* co-occur, and describes a bog site where several other orchid species coexist. I have observed only one population of *Platanthera ciliaris* that was not growing with the club moss (*Lycopodium*) known locally as running cedar, a species that also favors acidic soils.

When the soil chemistry is right, an area does not require a vast expanse of unspoiled wilderness to support impressive numbers of orchids. Once while house-hunting I stepped out the back door of one potential investment into the tiny patch of woods that had been left

Platanthera ciliaris grows alongside a road, with running cedar (*Lycopodium*) in the foreground. Monroe County, Tennessee, July.

untouched by the builder. It was clearly young second growth, dominated by some scraggly Virginia pines and numerous deciduous saplings, probably a pasture or cornfield less than thirty years before. Nevertheless, large patches of *Tipularia discolor* and *Goodyera pubescens* dotted the ground, littered with pine needles and leaves in late October. I considered buying the house just for the orchids but could not in the end justify the long commute to work.

Like sun exposure, soil pH may be difficult to change. Before planting hardy orchids in media directly in contact with the ground, have the soil tested, and choose plant species that grow within the pH range you can offer them. While amendments such as limestone or pine bark chips may be incorporated into the growing area to increase or decrease the pH, the effect is temporary. Unalterable conditions of the site, such as the underlying geology, will inexorably reassert themselves. Unless you are prepared to amend the soil indefinitely, the construction of enclosed beds filled with an appropriate growing medium may be the only option if the goal is to accommodate a wide variety of species.

NUTRIENTS

Tropical orchid enthusiasts often suggest fertilizing plants "weakly, weekly." Hardy orchids need even less feeding than this, and some require none at all. In the latter group are those that live in strongly acidic environments, where minimal levels of bacterial activity in the soil render the soil depauperate with regard to available nutrients. Species such as *Cypripedium acaule* have adapted to growing in poor soil and may actually be damaged by the application of chemical fertilizers. Further, the slow rate of decomposition in the acid environment required by these plants means that adding organic fertilizers, the effectiveness of which depends upon their decomposition, is a waste of time and money. The gradual breakdown of the compost itself provides adequate nutrients. Regular maintenance of the growing area requires simply adding an inch or so of new compost each fall. This material should consist of pine needles, bark chips, chopped pine cones, or similar materials derived from coniferous trees. Oak and beech leaves, sphagnum moss, and reindeer moss (really a lichen) may be incorporated into the mix, as these components frequently compose the soil in orchid-bearing woods.

"Bog orchids," the name I prefer to use for the taxonomically diverse but horticulturally similar collection of species that comprise the majority of all garden-worthy hardy orchids, may grow in mildly acidic, neutral, or mildly alkaline environments. Under any of these pH regimes, light feeding with artificial fertilizer about every two weeks during the growing season improves growth and flower production across the board. Bacterial activity in these substrates ensures a continuous low level of nutrients. You can also incorporate a timed-release fertilizer—for example, Osmocote—into the growing medium in spring. If, like me, you are both thrifty and somewhat lazy, you will find that adding organic fertilizers, including blood meal, bone meal, rock phosphate, and so forth, results in healthy plants and abundant flowers. For orchid growing, organic amendments should be applied at one-half to one-fourth the recommended rate on the product label. A single fall application works best, as this affords time for soil organisms to decompose the materials and release nutrients in a form available to the plants in time for the burst of growth in early spring.

Any garden that is to flourish needs a rich flora of soil microorganisms. Various formulas for orchid-growing media incorporate natural materials that introduce fungi and bacteria (see chapter 4 for more on mycorrhizal associations). I mentioned sphagnum moss, lichens, fallen leaves, and other materials. You can expect the best results from materials collected from natural orchid sites, such as in connection with a salvage dig. In any case, if you have access to appropriate organic amendments for your orchid beds, by all means include them.

COMPANION PLANTS

Choosing companions for hardy orchids must be done with care. Bear in mind that orchids favor sites where they have little competition. Be especially cautious about introducing plants with invasive tendencies—those with spreading roots or runners, for example, or those that drop an abundance of seeds—even if the invasiveness is mild. Mosses, the diminutive fern *Woodsia obtusa*, and the charming little Labrador violet (*Viola labradorica*) amicably join *Platanthera*, *Cypripedium*, *Spiranthes*, *Tipularia*, and *Dactylorhiza* in my bog garden. Slow growers, such as marsh marigold (*Caltha palustris*), irises (*Iris virginica*, *I. fulva*), and royal fern (*Osmunda regalis*), also grow in this bed, lending their drama to that of the orchids. Barbara's buttons (*Marshallia grandiflora*), a beautiful summer-blooming aster, may eventually prove too vigorous, but it can be easily removed and will not regrow from bits of root left behind. (I consider this bed a temporary home for all of the plants until the completion of landscaping around my house. It therefore contains a greater number and variety of plants than would otherwise be desirable.) Besides those mentioned, numerous familiar perennials can be grown alongside orchids. In my shade garden, three varieties of *Bletilla* keep company with *Begonia grandis* subsp. *evansiana*, *Brunnera macrophylla* 'Jack Frost', *Deparia petersonii*, *Dicentra spectabilis*, *Dryopteris cristata*, *D. erythrosora*, *D. marginalis*, *Hosta* cultivars, *Polygonatum odoratum*, *Sedum ternatum*, and *Tricyrtis hirta*

Viola pedata makes a perfect companion for *Cypripedium acaule,* blooming at the same time and in a complementary color.

'Miyazaki'. If a better companion for *Cypripedium acaule* than *Viola pedata* exists, I have yet to discover it.

Invasive, exotic pest plants pose a major threat not only to natural stands of orchids and other native plants but also to plants in the garden. Japanese honeysuckle, kudzu, privet, loosestrife, poison ivy, and many more introduced plant pests can overwhelm all efforts at control once they become established. Pest plant control gets high priority in any effort to establish a stand of native plants on an existing tract of woods. Obviously, all attempts to conserve or reestablish native plants on disturbed natural sites should proceed only after the presence of exotic pest plants has been evaluated and steps have been taken to eradicate them. Exotic pest plants pose such significant threats to native floras that I am tempted to add a few extra provisions to the conservation tips suggested in chapter 1, including tax credits for exotic pest plant removal on private property, more money for control of these plants on public lands, and more research into ways to avoid future problems. A stand of honeysuckle a mile from your house can provide thousands of seeds to be spread by birds to your backyard.

That said, don't let concern about pest plants scare you away from employing any of the thousands of perfectly harmless exotic plants available for the garden. Lack of significant natural enemies, vigorous growth, climbing or spreading habit, abundant seed production, and the ability to overcrowd native species characterize most pest plants. Most garden plants lack these qualities, although there are significant exceptions. Check with your local agricultural extension agent if you are unsure about the potential peskiness of any species you consider planting. Of course, always use common sense when pairing plants with delicate hardy orchids. Avoid those that might overwhelm, such as many common annuals.

SITING
Giving careful consideration to the physical location of your orchid plants with respect to the rest of the site will reward you with fewer plants damaged by pests, wind, pets, kids, and wildlife. Orchids are relatively safe from diseases and insects when they have proper grow-

ing conditions. Under the best of circumstances, however, physical damage can occur. In fact, physical damage has been the cause of most of my losses of hardy orchid plants over the years.

Common pests include snails and slugs. Leave the outdoor lights off and go out one warm spring evening with a flashlight to check for slugs crawling on patios and sidewalks. You can control these plant munchers by planting orchids away from any cool, dark, moist hiding places. Slugs can also be trapped with dishes of beer set out at dusk and dumped the next morning. In the case of a severe infestation, poisoned baits give good results. Regardless of the treatment, repeat it at intervals over several weeks to control the slug population. Thereafter, using beer traps should be sufficient.

Insect pests and diseases appear mostly on orchids that have been stressed by improper environmental conditions. White fly and aphids, both common greenhouse pests, succumb best to applications of insecticidal soap solution and an improvement in growing conditions. These critters have shown up only rarely on plants growing in my garden, and tend to be more of a threat to container-grown plants.

Wind and rain can damage the fragile leaves of orchid plants and ruin blooms and buds. The orchids should be sheltered from the prevailing winds by a building or windbreak, and protected from torrential rains by overhanging limbs or the leaves of companion plants.

If squirrels are abundant in your area, you may find they dig and uproot plants with infuriating frequency. After several years of unsuccessful attempts to thwart them, I came up with a workable solution. Shortly after plants emerge in spring, I give them a good sprinkling with cayenne pepper. I buy a large container for about $10 at a local restaurant supplier, and it lasts all season. I reapply the pepper about every week, or just after a rain, until the squirrels get the idea.

Locate the orchid garden away from the main flow of traffic in your yard to avoid accidental breakage. While such damage rarely kills the plant, blooming next season may be inhibited. Splinting broken plant parts, by the way, provides a satisfactory remedy for minor damage. As long as the broken part remains green, it can contribute to the plant's photosynthetic activity.

Dog urine, unfortunately, makes a good orchid herbicide, so you will need to shield the plants from your faithful pet. A physical barrier such as a fence or dense hedge works well. Similarly, if your cat uses the orchid bed as a litter box, you will need to scoop as soon as possible to avoid disaster. I find that a coarse mulch of pine bark chips deters cats.

Hardy orchids respond well to horticultural practices that provide the conditions they encounter in nature, the important parameters being moisture content of the growing medium, sun exposure, humidity, pH, nutrient availability, proper selection of companion plants, and correct siting.

Our native orchids are "rare" only because their preferred habitats are unusual and are too often appropriated by humans, who alter the environment beyond a point the orchids can tolerate. Low-lying, level, well-watered sites are ideal for agriculture. Excess water can be channeled away from development projects with culverts and canals. Streams can be rerouted with impunity. Bogs can be drained, leaving rich, level plains that can be economically farmed or otherwise developed. All this activity results in the supply of orchid habitat literally drying up. Natural stands of some orchids may be relegated to remote or inaccessible regions, such as rugged mountains, and the plants develop a reputation for being rare and mysterious. Thus, people seldom think of including them in their gardens. With only a little encouragement, native orchids (or their hardy, exotic relatives) can be grown successfully in a backyard garden, though not in the same soil mix nor in the same bed with many of the more familiar flowers.

As methods for commercial-scale production of hardy orchids develop, the plants will become more widely available. Americans have fallen in love with tropical orchids; ample reason exists for them to fall for the hardy ones, also. Horticulturists have already created numerous hybrids in many genera, and a few intergeneric ones. Natural hybrids of *Platanthera*, such as *P. ×andrewsii* (*P. lacera* × *P. psycodes*), demonstrate clearly the potential for many new and beautiful hybrids that exists within this genus. For specialty farmers, production of hardy orchids may prove to be an attractive niche industry. Temperate-zone orchids offer enormous horticultural potential, if only we can over-come the longstanding prejudice against growing them.

Enjoying Hardy Orchids at Home

Most hardy orchid species are far less adaptable than familiar garden perennials. They therefore require a commitment from the gardener and are not for everyone. Growing plants in prepared beds or contain-ers of artificial media is the best overall approach, unless you already have plants of the same species growing naturally on the site. Installa-tion of suitable beds does not involve major expense and can be ac-complished by anyone who knows how to use a hammer, but an in-vestment of money and time will be required. If you are going for an inexpensive, low-maintenance garden, a wide range of hardy orchids may not be for you.

Lobelia cardinalis, Platanthera ciliaris, P. integrilabia, and *Pontederia cordata* share one of my sunny bog gardens.

In fact, the best advice I can offer a beginner is this: specialize. Start with one or two genera and learn the basics of hardy orchid cultivation before attempting more demanding species. Read the species accounts in the chapters that follow, and choose those whose needs you can most easily meet. After a season or two of blooms, you can try a more demanding specimen.

CONSTRUCTING AN OUTDOOR GROWING BED

If you happen to be blessed with a suitably shaded site with good drainage, preparing a growing bed for hardy orchids can be as simple as dumping out a few bags of mulch and other materials from a DIY store. Orchids that typically grow in areas dominated by coniferous trees—*Cypripedium acaule*, *Goodyera pubescens*, *Platanthera ciliaris*, and a few others—grow well in raised mounds of growing medium put in place without excavation or tilling.

Underneath a white pine (*Pinus strobus*) growing beside my house, we spread out a circle of landscape fabric at a radius of about 6 feet from the tree trunk. The fabric was secured with aluminum staples and a border of plastic edging set into a trench. Digging consisted only of creating the trench. Once the fabric was securely in place, we added 3 inches of pine bark "nuggets" averaging about the size of a nickel. Next came a second 3-inch layer, consisting of partially composted pine bark fines.

Plantings consisted of *Cypripedium acaule* and *Goodyera pubescens* salvaged from the site described in chapter 1. We settled the orchids and a few companion plants in this layer at about the same depth they were growing in the woods—that is, with the tip of the growth bud about an inch below the surface in the case of *C. acaule*, and with the creeping stem barely covered in the case of *G. pubescens*. We added moss, lichens, and composted plant debris from the collecting site. After watering everything in, we mulched with an inch of pine needles.

The plants thrived during the summer after planting, with some producing blooms. The white pine added additional mulch in early fall, including a few cones. By using appropriate media, almost any area can be turned into an orchid bed using this technique.

Another option is to excavate a bed below ground level to contain the growing medium, but this approach requires considerably more effort. To ensure adequate drainage, a deep layer of coarse gravel, and in some situations a plastic drain line, must be incorporated into the design. These features require additional earth removal, leading to the issue of what to do with the soil from the hole. Avoiding underground utility pipes and cables is another concern. On anything other than a very modest scale, a project like this may call for the advice of a professional landscaper. Do-it-yourselfers will find building a raised bed easier and cheaper.

Cypripedium acaule blooms in my garden the second spring after transplanting.

Covered with a circle of landscape fabric, the area around this white pine (*Pinus strobus*) is about to become an orchid bed.

Adding the growing medium readies the bed for planting.

The completed bed with *Cypripedium acaule* plants in place.

CONSTRUCTING A BOG GARDEN

Orchidists have Holman (1976) to thank for designing and testing the bog garden method for growing hardy orchids. I have used some variation of the basic design to create growing places for every species of hardy orchid in my collection, with the exception of *Bletilla* and the species that love strongly acid soil. Orchid growers familiar with *Phragmipedium*, a genus of tropical slipper orchids, will quickly get the point. Like this cousin, many cypripediums, to choose but one example, flourish in a growing medium constantly replenished with moisture from below. Growers display spectacular specimens of *Phragmipedium besseae* that have been grown in pots set in a dish of water. The reservoir ensures that the growing medium will never dry out completely, and the composition of the medium ensures that it will remain loose, fluffy, and well oxygenated. The Holman bog garden simply accomplishes the same thing on a much larger scale.

In its simplest and most easily constructed form, the bog garden consists of a rectangular frame made of 2-by-12-foot pressure-treated lumber (or another material impervious to rot). Three 8-foot pieces will make a 4-by-8-foot bed with only one cut. Square up the pieces and secure them with 3-inch exterior wood screws. Set the box in position in the garden.

It is extremely helpful to have a level site covered with landscape fabric cut a few inches larger than the bed. You may need to bring in soil, sand, or gravel to level the site, or to do a bit of excavation by hand. For a 4-by-8-foot bed, this should not be too onerous, however. Once the bed enclosure is in place, use a carpenter's level to make sure it sits level in both directions. Having the bed level ensures even distribution of moisture throughout the growing medium it will eventually contain.

When you are satisfied with the placement of the bed, cut a piece of plastic sheeting 6 by 10 feet. Depending upon how long you want the

The first step in assembling a raised bog garden bed involves assembling a wood frame to contain the growing media.

bed to last, the sheeting can be anything from 6-mil polyethylene film to a 45-mil rubber roofing membrane. The best compromise between cost and durability may prove to be 32-mil polyvinyl chloride, which is sold at DIY stores and garden centers for lining garden ponds. Six-mil polyethylene will last only two or three seasons but can be used for a temporary bed. Roofing membrane, by contrast, is nearly indestructible.

Regardless of the material chosen, line the bed with the plastic, centering the sheet in the bottom and smoothing it toward the sides. Make neat folds at the corners and staple them in place with a heavy-duty staple gun. You want to end up with the plastic lining extending at least

Line the frame with plastic, stapling it in place.

Trim away excess plastic with a razor.

Add a layer of filler material about 6 inches deep.

halfway up the sides of the bed all around. There should be plenty of excess, which can be carefully trimmed away after stapling the lining in place. Don't worry about doing a perfect job, as the edges will be hidden by the compost. Do make sure the top edge of the liner is trimmed evenly all around, as, again, this ensures even distribution of moisture within the bed.

Directly above the edge of the liner in several spots drill a 1-inch-diameter hole using an electric drill fitted with a spade bit. This provides extra drainage in times of heavy rainfall. Arrange the holes in an attractive pattern, if that suits your taste.

Various materials have been suggested for filling the liner to provide a waterlogged reservoir to irrigate the upper half of the bed. Having tried several, I find shredded mulch made from the southern bald cy-

Spread the filler material evenly in the bottom of the bed.

press to be the most satisfactory material. It is lightweight, does not rot, and is sold in bags at garden centers. That said, any nondecomposing, relatively inert material will do. If orchids preferring neutral to alkaline conditions are to be planted in the bed, crushed limestone should be the material of choice. Sixteen cubic feet of filler will be required.

After filling the reservoir, flood the liner to overflowing with a garden hose. Water should pour from each of your drainage holes before you shut off the hose. If you are using a filler material that absorbs water, such as the cypress mulch, allow it to sit overnight to become satu-

Flood the filler material with water and allow it to soak overnight before proceeding with construction.

rated. Obviously, if you are using a nonabsorbent material such as gravel, you can skip this step.

Another 16 cubic feet of orchid growing medium will be required to fill the bog bed. You can use any of the following media, depending upon the orchids you plan to grow:

CRIBB & BAILES (1989) **Australian terrestrial mix**
Two parts sharp, gritty sand (could substitute perlite)
One part sterilized loam
One part screened pine bark fines
2 teaspoons each blood meal and bone meal per 2 gallons of mix

CRIBB & BAILES (1989) **bog mix**
  for *Platanthera*
Three parts coarse, gritty sand or perlite (must use sand for outdoor beds, as perlite will float to the surface eventually)
Two parts sphagnum peat
Chopped pine needles for mulch

CRIBB & BAILES (1989) **terrestrial mix**
Two parts sterilized clay loam
Two parts sharp, gritty sand (could substitute perlite)
One part screened beech or oak leaf mould
One part screened pine bark fines
1 teaspoon each blood meal and bone meal per 2 gallons of mix

DURKEE (2000) *Cypripedium acaule* **mix**
Two parts partially composted pine bark fines
One part chopped sphagnum moss

PHILLIPS (1985) **woodland wildflower mix**
  for *Aplectrum* and *Bletilla*
Two parts partially composted pine bark fines
Two parts peat moss
One part perlite
19 ounces dolomitic limestone per 4.5 cubic feet of mix
2 tablespoons Osmocote 14-14-14 per 4.5 cubic feet of mix (optional)

TULLOCK *Cypripedium acaule* mix
   for *C. acaule, Disa,* and Australian species
Two parts partially composted pine bark fines
One part peat moss

TULLOCK **general purpose mix**
   for *Bletilla, Calopogon, Platanthera, Pleione, Spiranthes,* and *Tipularia*
Two parts partially composted pine bark fines
One part long-fiber sphagnum moss
One part perlite

TULLOCK **general purpose mix with lime**
   for *Galearis, Cypripedium parviflorum, C. pubescens* and *C. reginae*
Two parts partially composted pine bark fines
One part long-fiber sphagnum moss
One part perlite
1 tablespoon pelletized limestone per 6- to 8-inch pot

Plant the orchids so that their crowns lie just at the surface of the bog bed.

The completed framed bog bed two months after planting.

Mix the components in batches in a wheelbarrow before adding the medium to the bed. Do not risk puncturing the plastic liner by using metal tools in the bed itself. The medium should be light enough to permit planting with a hand spade or even your gloved hands. Flood the bed again until water drains from the holes and you are satisfied that the medium is thoroughly moistened. The bed is now ready to plant.

It is easy to see that the basic bog bed can be elaborated upon in any number of ways to create a more dramatic garden display or to integrate with existing landscaping. You can excavate for the reservoir, install drainage pipes for the necessary overflow, and use anything from plastic to concrete for the liner. As long as the basic design provides for 6 inches of growing medium atop a permanently flooded reservoir, the method will work. As with the simpler growing bed, more elaborate installations may require professional assistance.

Constructing an in-ground bog bed requires digging, and lining the excavation with heavy plastic.

With filler material in place, this in-ground bog waits to receive growing medium and plants.

The completed bog garden, one year and two months after planting.

The bog garden after two years and four months of growth.

GROWING HARDY ORCHIDS IN CONTAINERS

All kinds of containers may substitute for constructed beds. For a small collection, this may be the best way to go, especially if you have some spare refrigerator space. My local DIY store sells a black polypropylene tub for about $20 that holds 15–20 gallons. Its intended use is as a garden pond liner, and it is impervious to decomposition. Being black in color, it is easily hidden and will not degrade in sunlight. Best of all, it is about a foot deep. Simply drilling a series of holes around the perimeter about halfway up produces a minibog. Ten or fifteen cypripediums and as many as twenty platantheras can be accommodated in this simple arrangement, which in all respects (apart from size) mirrors the larger bog beds. I suggest limiting each container to a single orchid species. Large nursery containers with drainage holes in the bottom can similarly be used to hold orchids that do not require a constantly moist growing medium, such as *Cypripedium acaule* and *Bletilla*.

Individual orchid plants can be grown in pots like those commonly used for tropical orchids, of either plastic or terra cotta. For orchids that prefer constant moisture, the pots can be set in a pan or dish of water. The main drawback to container growing of bog orchids on this scale stems from the high likelihood that the whole thing will dry out during hot weather. I prefer the 20-gallon garden pond liner for these species.

Regardless of the species being grown, choose a container that will accommodate the roots without crowding. Cypripediums, for example, have an upright growth point or points about the size of a pencil and up to $1\frac{1}{2}$ inches in length. Radiating out from this central point are thick white roots that resemble tough spaghetti. Most plants have relatively few roots. A shallow, circular depression that allows the roots to be comfortably spread with their tips slightly lower than the center of the plant works best. Cypripediums, therefore, call for an 8- to 10-inch-diameter squat pot that nurserymen call an "azalea pan" or "mum pot." Platantheras, on the other hand, have fingerlike rhizomes, a few fleshy roots, and one or more strongly vertical growth points. Consequently, a deeper pot works best for them.

I find that container-grown orchids are often top-heavy, which leaves them vulnerable to wind or slight disturbances. This condition can be remedied by choosing a relatively shallow, wide container that tends to lower the center of gravity of the whole plant. Obviously, terra cotta or pottery works better than lighter-weight materials such as plastic or fiberglass for this purpose. Stones can be placed in the bottom of the pot to add weight.

Regardless of the species or type of container, all hardy orchids should be removed from their pots and stored under refrigeration during the winter months. Storage can be done anytime after the leaves die naturally but should take place before a hard freeze develops. Alternatively, dormancy can be induced by chilling the plant, pot and all, in the refrigerator for a few days. After emptying the container, carefully rinse each plant free of most of the adhering debris and pack it in a suitable storage medium held in plastic food-storage containers. For orchids that need constant moisture, the best storage medium is long-fiber sphagnum moss that has been thoroughly moistened and wrung out. Choose a container of suitable size and shape, and place the orchid in a more or less natural growth position atop a layer of sphagnum. Gently tuck more sphagnum, first around the growth point, then the rest of the plant. Use extreme care to avoid damage to the growth point.

Write the name of the plant and the date on the container with a nursery marker, and store the container in a refrigerator set to 35°F–38°F. The cheapest containers I have found are those clear plastic "clamshells" from delis and supermarkets. They come in many sizes and are amazingly durable. Simply wash them in soap and water and save them for storing your orchids in the fall. The clamshell design assures that the lid won't get lost, and since they are free with the food you buy, you can afford to toss them after a season. I do recommend tossing them, by the way, because reusing storage containers may spread disease to your plants. If you must reuse containers, sterilize them with a solution of 1 cup (8 fluid ounces) of household bleach in a 5-gallon bucket of water. Pouring boiling water over the sphagnum and allowing it to cool to room temperature before use is also a good idea.

A few orchids, such as *Cypripedium acaule*, *Bletilla*, and the summer-dormant species such as *Ophrys*, should be stored in a dry medium. Horticultural peat moss, sterilized by baking in a 250°F oven for an hour and allowing to cool to room temperature, works well and is universally available. Place a layer of peat in the bottom of the container, arrange the plant on top, mist the plant with a little water, and cover with more peat before closing the lid.

Goodyera presents a special case, as it is evergreen. If you grow goodyeras in containers, sink them in the ground or in a thick layer of mulch to protect the roots better during winter.

Creating an artificial habitat for hardy orchids does not present major challenges to the experienced gardener, and the skills required can be quickly mastered by any novice. Depending upon the size of your collection and your resources, hardy orchids can occupy a few pots on the patio or a sweeping wildflower garden under mature trees. The principles for constructing a strongly acidic, constantly moist, or rich woodland environment remain constant irrespective of the size of the project.

HARDY ORCHIDS AS CUT FLOWERS

All the hardy orchids I have grown make excellent cut flowers. Unless you desire seed production, cutting the blooms will not harm the plants and may even cause them to devote more energy to developing the rootstock that will host next year's bigger and better show.

An orchid's life in the vase can be greatly prolonged by the addition of a floral preservative. My favorite florist, Scott Morrell, has offered me several suggestions regarding floral preservatives. The objective is to feed the flower while inhibiting bacterial growth. Most commercial formulas, like the little packets that come with supermarket flowers, include citric acid, a bit of sugar, and sometimes traces of an oxidant, such as sodium peroxide, to inhibit bacteria. Have no fear: you could drink the stuff and it would do no harm, other than perhaps upsetting your stomach. However, rather than purchasing these products, consider adding a shot glass of lemon-lime soda or ginger ale to a pint of water—a refreshing cocktail for cut flowers. Or just set the flowers in club soda and add a squeeze of lemon and a pinch of sugar.

Propagation
of Hardy Orchids

ONCE YOU HAVE ESTABLISHED HARDY ORCHID PLANTS blooming profusely each season under your care, your attention may be drawn to the prospect of increasing their numbers. Propagation of hardy terrestrial orchids can range from childishly simple to fiendishly difficult. Some, such as *Bletilla* species, can simply be chopped into pieces and replanted. Others, such as cypripediums, which are nearly impossible to divide, must be grown from seed, a notoriously slow and demanding procedure.

The majority of tropical orchids, though often easily divided, are propagated via laboratory techniques and require three to seven years from seed to flower. Why then are the hardy species not also in commercial production? Unfortunately, the horticultural world has been told for years that hardy orchids cannot be grown successfully and that revealing techniques for growing them will encourage digging of wild plants. I wonder why this argument has not been applied to the countless other wildflower species available in the trade, including many now considered standard garden perennials. The surge in the popularity of

Sarracenia (pitcher plants) occurred unaccompanied by fears of depredations on the bogs of North Carolina's coastal plain. *Sarracenia* takes roughly as long to produce as do many orchids. The plants at my local nursery cost no more than other good-quality perennials. Buying propagated *Sarracenia* simply presents fewer obstacles and requires far less time than slogging through a mucky lowland bog, burdened with tools and slapping at insects. Propagation of rare plant species raises consciousness about plant biodiversity in general, provides opportunities for including more wild species in public plantings and gardens, allows hobby gardeners to make their mistakes and enjoy their triumphs without concern about environmental damage, and creates a large pool of plants for research and habitat restoration.

The general principles and guidelines presented in this chapter are aimed at assisting more avid enthusiasts to develop better methods for propagating their favorites. In my experience, the most horticulturally desirable hardy orchids correspond to the most difficult to propagate. Murphy's Law of hardy terrestrial orchid propagation reads, "The more you like the parents, the fewer offspring you will get." *Bletilla* seems to be the sole exception to this rule, not only performing well in the garden but also being easy to divide and growing quickly from seed.

Seed Germination

Unlike those of some fussier species, seeds of *Bletilla* and *Aplectrum* germinate reasonably well on sphagnum moss or compost (Glick 2000, Riley 1999). This technique might be worth a try for other common woodland species such as *Goodyera*.

To prepare a sterile germination pot, wash a 6-inch plastic azalea pan in hot soapy water. You will also need a piece of window glass (grind or sand the edges to avoid cuts) or clear, rigid plastic large enough to cover the pot. Wash the cover along with the pot, and rinse it with distilled water to help prevent spotting, which will make it hard to observe the germinating seeds without removing the cover. Set the cover aside while preparing the germination medium.

Fill the pot with chopped long-fiber sphagnum moss that has been carefully picked over to remove debris and then soaked in distilled water. Squeeze out most of the water before filling the pot, leaving about a half inch of head space. To maintain aeration and drainage, take care not to pack the moss too firmly. Bring a gallon of distilled water to a rolling boil in an enameled stainless steel or Pyrex stockpot. Set the pot of sphagnum moss in the sink. Carefully pour boiling water over the moss, making sure to wet the entire surface. Use all the water to ensure a thorough job. While the pot drains, wipe the cover with a paper towel moistened with rubbing alcohol, allow it to dry for a few moments, and place it over the still steaming pot. Allow the prepared pot to cool to room temperature, sprinkle the orchid seeds over the surface, cover, and set it outside in a sheltered spot (or, preferably, in an alpine greenhouse) to germinate.

Glick (2000) suggests using woodland growing mix instead of sphagnum for *Aplectrum* seeds, adding a thin covering of sand to deter molds and algae. He recommends placing the pot, uncovered, in a convenient spot in the outdoor garden. Personally, I prefer more control than this over conditions of germination and early growth. Orchid seedlings are more fragile than mature plants and, in my experience, need careful attention.

The next rung up the ladder of complexity in hardy orchid seed propagation techniques is the use of artificial, agar-based media in flasks for germination and early growth. While "sterilizing" pots with boiling water in reality only pasteurizes them without killing 100 percent of the living organisms present, flasked media are truly sterile, having been exposed to pressurized steam in an autoclave. The only sources of potential contamination of the flask, therefore, are the seeds themselves and any utensils employed to transfer them from pod to flask.

Seed laboratories able to accept mature pods and grow them out for a fee are commonly advertised for tropical orchids but remain few and far between for hardy species. Nevertheless, if you have the time and space, you can germinate orchid seeds in flasks at home.

While I have not yet undertaken orchid propagation in vitro, I did spend many years working in microbiological laboratories and am capable of explaining sterile technique. You will need an impervious work surface that can be easily disinfected, good task lighting, a razor blade, and a flame for sterilizing utensils. The latter requirement is easily met by a small propane torch available at any hardware store. (Always read and follow the manufacturer's instructions and safety recommendations when using it.)

According to practitioners, using mature, brown seed pods that have already split open to disperse their seeds not only greatly increases the likelihood of contamination of the flask but also increases the time for germination to commence. This occurs because the mature seed coat contains germination inhibitors, designed by evolution to ensure that germination occurs on an appropriate schedule consistent with the climate of the orchid's native habitat. Unopened pods, filled with "green" though nevertheless mature seeds, offer the best chances for success. The timing of seed collection, therefore, becomes crucially important. Ripe green pods often exhibit browning but remain intact. The seeds inside lack pigmentation and will separate from each other with relative ease.

Have all the equipment and materials assembled and ready when you collect the pods. Keep track of which plants provided seeds for which flask, if you plan any serious breeding or research. A nursery marker, available at any garden center, can be used to write directly on the flasks. Disinfect the work surface by wiping it down with a mild solution of household bleach, $1/2$ ounce per quart of water. Also prepare a small dish or jar of this solution, and dip the pod into it, swishing it around several times while holding it with a pair of tweezers, the tip of which should be sterilized in the flame before picking up the pod. The bleach solution should kill any contaminants hitchhiking on the pod.

Sterilize the razor blade by holding it in the flame for a few seconds, and then slit the pod open to reveal the seeds. Using the tip of the blade, transfer seeds to flasks, spreading them out as evenly as possible on the agar surface. When you remove the cap, hold the flask at an angle to prevent airborne microorganisms from entering. Pass the mouth of the flask through the flame before dumping in the seeds. Flame the mouth of the flask again before replacing the cap. The more dexterous gardener may readily master the technique of holding the flask in the left hand (for a right-hander) and removing the cap with the heel and third and fourth fingers of the right hand, leaving the other two fingers and the thumb free to manipulate the blade carrying the seeds. If you find that you must lay things on the tabletop in order to proceed, lay them on a sterile surface such as a gauze pad or a sterilized serving tray.

After the seeds are successfully transferred, the flasks will require various treatments to promote germination. Numerous factors influence seed germination (see, for example, Allen 1996). Two of the most important are seed dormancy and the possibility of overgrowth by contaminating microorganisms. The latter problem is best avoided by scrupulously adhering to sterile technique, as there is not much to be done once a mold has started growing in the germination flask. Seed dormancy presents more formidable obstacles. Dormancy ensures that germination will occur at the proper time of year and only under circumstances favorable to seedling development. This makes good evolutionary sense. The orchid, having expended so much effort to produce thousands of seeds, cannot afford to waste them by having them germinate inappropriately, since the odds of any given seed falling on just the right substrate and encountering a suitable fungal partner are already slim. As a result of selection pressure, hardy orchid seeds may require various combinations of light, moisture, temperature, or other environmental variables in order to germinate. Ever wonder how a wide-ranging plant "knows" that it is fine to germinate in March in the South but not until May in Minnesota? The plant's germination requirements are aligned with key environmental changes that occur with the cycle of the seasons. Discovering the appropriate parameters is a considerable challenge, but fortunately has been accomplished for the majority of horticulturally desirable species. *Arethusa bulbosa*, for example, requires chilling for three or four months in complete darkness and with abundant moisture (Yanetti 1996).

Once germination is accomplished, growth rates vary by species. The orchid embryo develops into a structure called the protocorm and may remain in this stage for months or years before developing a leaf. Prior to doing so under cultivation, many species require a cold period to fool them into thinking winter has come and gone and the time for making leaves has arrived. Usually this is accomplished by removing seedlings from the flask when they have small roots and leaf scales, refrigerating them, and potting them in growth medium once a green leaf appears. The length of the chilling period varies with the orchid species. In *Cypripedium acaule*, a slow-growing species, this whole process can take two years to complete.

With regard to the choice of medium for germinating hardy terrestrial orchid seeds, Svante Malmgren's (1996) recipe works well. It includes the following:

Calcium phosphate, $Ca_3(PO_4)_2$	50–100 mg
Magnesium sulfate, $MgSO_4 \cdot 7\,H_2O$	50–100 mg
Potassium dihydrogen phosphate, KH_2PO_4	50–100 mg
Sugar	10 g (in sowing medium)
	15–20 g (in growing medium)
Agar-agar	6 g
Pineapple juice	10–25 ml
Amino acid mixture	To give about 300 mg amino acids
Vitamin mixture	One or two drops
Tap water	1 liter
Charcoal (horticultural)	About 0.5 g

A few comments about this recipe are in order. Malmgren (in Anderson 1996) reports using the medium successfully for germination and grow-out of *Cypripedium*, *Dactylorhiza*, *Gymnadenia*, *Nigritella*, *Ophrys*, *Orchis*, and *Platanthera*. Adding 2–5 mg kinetine was reported as being necessary for some *Cypripedium*, while *Dactylorhiza* did better with 50–100 mg of ammonium nitrate added to the basic medium. For the nitrogen source, Malmgren, a physician, uses Vamin, an amino acid solution used in European hospitals. A lysine tablet from the drugstore could substitute, as the exact amino acid composition probably does not matter. For the vitamin mixture, Malmgren uses Soluvit, a vitamin solution used in hospitals. Aquarium shops sell a liquid vitamin supplement for fish foods that should do as well. With the exception of the amino acid solution and vitamin mixture, the components should be easy to obtain, although you may have problems getting ammonium nitrate, as it has been used as an explosive for terrorist bombings. Check with a pharmacist about the American equivalents of Vamin and Soluvit and about the other components not found in the grocery store. Magnesium sulfate is Epsom salt. Agar is available from Asian markets and natural food groceries.

For the hardy terrestrial orchids described as relatively easy to germinate, including *Aplectrum*, *Bletilla*, and perhaps a few others, flasked media normally used for tropical orchid seed germination can be bought ready-made from mail-order suppliers. (See "Suppliers and Organizations.")

Extensive information concerning germination requirements and media for hardy terrestrial orchid seed propagation can be found in the conference proceedings of the 1996 North American Native Terrestrial Orchid Conference, edited by Carol Allen, including works by Anderson, Chu and Mudge, Gill, Light, Malmgren, Steele, Stoutamire, Whitlow, Yanetti, and Zettler.

Perhaps the most exciting aspect of research into hardy terrestrial orchid propagation has been the use of fungal isolates to assist symbiotically in seed germination (Zettler 1996). In one experiment, after sowing seed on a simple medium containing 2.5 grams of oatmeal and 7 grams of agar in a liter of water, the flasks were inoculated with fungi—typically, though not in all cases, using those isolated from the same species of orchid as that being germinated. Germination rates as high as 73 percent were obtained using these methods, although the average rate was about 50 percent, and three species, *Corallorhiza odontorhiza*, *Isotria medeoloides*, and *Tipularia discolor*, failed to germinate at all. *Goodyera pubescens* and *Spiranthes cernua* var. *cernua* germinated better than 70 percent with a fungal isolate from *Platanthera ciliaris*. The other species successfully germinated were *Platanthera ciliaris*, *P. clavellata*, *P. cristata*, *P. integrilabia*, and *Spiranthes odorata* (*S. cernua* var. *odorata*).

Like tropical orchid seedlings, hardy orchid seedlings are more delicate than their mature counterparts. Given proper culture, which usually means treating them like adults only with more attention, maturation into a blooming-size plant can take as little as two to as long as seven years. The average nursery-grown hardy orchid, therefore, will be about five years old before it flowers.

Plant Tissue Culture

One of the many incorrect assertions about hardy terrestrial orchids made in some generalized wildflower books is that propagated plants are available from "tissue culture laboratories." This statement is apparently intended to imply how difficult cultivation of terrestrial orchids may prove to be, should the foolhardy gardener attempt it. Despite the fact that thousands of common horticultural subjects, from ferns to tropical orchids to poinsettias, are routinely produced via plant tissue culture (or meristem propagation, as orchidists call the procedure), and despite the technique's having been around since the 1960s, hardy terrestrial orchids remain among the plants that have *not* successfully been produced via tissue culture. I suspect many cases are similar to that of *Spiranthes cernua* var. *odorata* 'Chadd's Ford', which, according to grower Barry Glick (personal communication), failed to adapt to tissue culture because the orchid cells could not be satisfactorily separated from fungal contaminants that subsequently overgrew the culture medium. Having effective tissue culture methods for hardy terrestrial orchids would be of great benefit, allowing many plants to be produced with less effort than seed propagation. Tissue culture also would make possible the wider dissemination of horticulturally desirable cultivars and hybrids that can at present only be cloned via the slow, old-fashioned method of vegetative division. Research into methods for tissue culture propagation of hardy terrestrial orchids may offer hope for species facing extinction, enabling as it would the preservation of many genetic varieties of the threatened species.

Seed propagation of all but a few of the orchid species considered in this book typically requires considerable expense and effort, lending itself better to a determined commercial venture than a backyard grower's weekend project. Nevertheless, propagating hardy terrestrial orchids from seed on a small scale can hardly be considered out of reach for the dedicated enthusiast who understands the necessary techniques and who is endowed with sufficient patience. The rest of us will have to depend upon others for seed-grown plants. Vegetative propagation does work well for many species, notably *Bletilla*, *Spiranthes*, and *Platanthera*, and involves little in the way of technical expertise apart from common sense and basic gardening knowledge.

Transplanting Hardy Orchids

Numerous occasions have presented themselves, or been forced upon me, that necessitated relocating the orchids in my collection. Friends have offered plants from their own gardens, my choice of appropriate placement turned out to be a poor one, or I moved to another house. I have also participated in several orchid salvage projects. As a result, I have transplanted orchids in all stages of growth from dormancy to full bloom, and have seldom lost a single plant. Of the hundreds of *Cypripedium acaule* plants moved in the salvage dig described in chapter 1, only three or four failed to resprout the following spring. As with tropical orchids, it is better to go ahead and transplant than to allow a plant to remain in undesirable circumstances in the garden.

Winter dormancy offers the best opportunity for transplanting, and the majority of mail-order hardy orchids will be shipped during their natural dormant period. All of those with which I have experience store successfully under refrigeration. Moisture content of the storage medium plays a significant role in determining how the plants fare. Bog orchids generally need to be stored damp, while most others prefer a dry medium, such as peat moss, as you might use in storing gladiolus corms.

For readily divided types, such as *Bletilla*, division can be done successfully anytime after the flowers fade, and transplanting nearly always succeeds. *Spiranthes*, which produces plantlets at the tips of elongated runners, can easily be increased by removing and replanting the offspring in early to mid spring. During dormancy, side shoots that form on *Platanthera* rhizomes can be carefully detached, then planted separately in early spring. If you are exceedingly fortunate, a *Cypripedium* will develop enough well-rooted side shoots to tempt you to divide it with a sharp knife. I for one have not yet worked up the nerve to try this on one of my larger plants.

Be especially careful about damaging the white, fleshy roots of any orchids you move. Broken roots are subject to infection and may account for many recorded plant losses (*Horticulture* 2000). Application of powdered sulfur to broken areas may help prevent this problem.

Pleione formosana, corm.

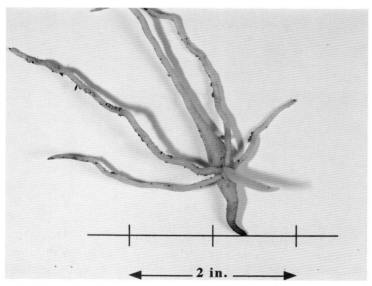

Platanthera integrilabia, dormant rootstock.

Galearis spectabilis, dormant rootstock.

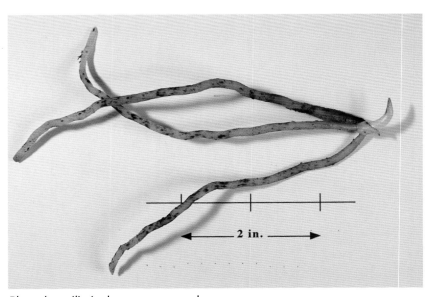

Platanthera ciliaris, dormant rootstock.

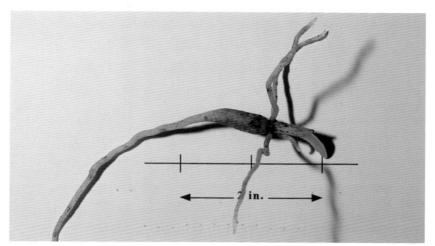

Dactylorhiza fuchsii, dormant rootstock.

Cypripedium reginae, dormant rootstock.

Cypripedium acaule, dormant rootstock. The plant on the left grew in an outdoor bed, while the one on the right grew in a container.

And so we come full circle. Hardy terrestrial orchids can be successfully cultivated and enjoyed even in backyard gardens. Many of them already reach enthusiastic gardeners as the product of nursery propagation by seed and division, and even the home-based amateur may attempt seed propagation with a reasonable expectation of success. All of this can happen without the slightest threat to any natural orchid population. On the contrary, highway projects and other development alone might provide many plants for research and the establishment of protected populations of local genetic stocks. Granted, where large or otherwise unusual stands of rare plants occur, the impact of development on the local ecology, represented by the orchids but shared by every organism in the habitat, must be carefully weighed against any public good that might be derived from the destruction of the habitat. The questions of where to draw appropriate lines in such matters and how to manage our plant resources for the future present significant challenges to policy makers at all levels—community, municipality, state, region, and ultimately the entire country. With any luck we will have the wisdom to try some new approaches to plant conservation, and in particular to recruit the amateur enthusiast in that endeavor.

Mycorrhizal Associations and Hardy Orchids

MANY AUTHORS HAVE SUGGESTED THAT, DESPITE their desirability, terrestrial orchids will always present considerable difficulty in culture. Some will undoubtedly remain difficult because of their resolute dependence upon a precise, hard-to-duplicate set of ecological conditions. Others will be found more amenable to cultivation as laboratory- and nursery-propagated plants become more widely available, and as horticulturists have a supply of plants with which to experiment. Hybridization can be expected to produce new varieties more amenable to cultivation than their parents.

When trying to explain the difficulty of growing hardy terrestrial orchids, authors frequently cite the presumed requirement of a symbiotic fungus that lives in association with the orchid's roots. Botanists refer to these fungi as mycorrhizae and speak of a mycorrhizal association between fungus and plant. Although a large percentage of all vascular plants develop mycorrhizal associations, orchids have carried this relationship to the extreme and depend absolutely upon the fungus for the successful development of germinating seedlings. As adults, however, only a minority of orchid species completely depend upon the fungus.

Shortly after germinating, an orchid seedling must establish a mycorrhizal association in order to obtain nourishment, because orchid evolution has resulted in loss of the endosperm. All other seed plants produce an endosperm containing stored food for the germinating embryo. Streamlining the seed down to the bare essentials allows it to be carried great distances by wind and water. When a seed is deposited, by sheer luck, in a location having appropriate environmental conditions and a suitable fungus, it can germinate and grow. The fungus digests organic matter, making nutrients available for the tiny orchid. Because the odds of any one seed landing in precisely the right circumstances are small, orchid plants compensate by producing thousands of seeds from each pollinated flower.

The phenomenon of fungal symbiosis explains why both tropical and hardy orchid seeds grow on nutrient media in flasks when produced commercially. Although it is possible to germinate seeds and subsequently grow them symbiotically by "infecting" them with a fungal partner, the procedure is seldom employed for commercial production. Virtually all orchid seedlings are therefore grown on artificial media.

No one who studies orchids argues that the fungal symbiosis can be dispensed with for seed germination under natural conditions, but what happens when the orchid develops roots and is able to absorb nutrients directly from its surroundings? We know from millions of examples that tropical orchids can be successfully grown without special concern for their mycorrhizae. After a period of time in the flask, orchid seedlings are planted out in the media that they will grow in for the rest of their lives, usually nearly sterile mixtures of bark, peat moss, perlite, or other relatively inert components that supply little in the way of nutrition. However, provided with the right proportions of light, water, humidity, and fertilizer, orchids thrive for years with no apparent fungal partner. In fact, growers often apply fungicides to orchid plants in an effort to control disease.

Terrestrial orchids, on the other hand, have been regarded as being dependent upon fungal symbionts beyond the seedling stage. Evidence, however, suggests that this may not be the case, at least for purposes of successful horticulture. Even horticulturally difficult species such as *Arethusa bulbosa* have been grown successfully from seed to flower under sterile conditions (Yanetti 1996).

A classic case of finickiness in cultivation attributed to the inability to establish a mycorrhizal association is *Cypripedium acaule*, considered to be among the most challenging species. However, its requirement for a soil pH of 4–5, around that of vinegar, may have more to do with cultural failures than lack of a fungus. Further, an article in *Horticulture* (2000) suggests that collected plants, whose roots are cut or broken by rough handling, are more difficult to establish because the damaged root system develops rot. Gardeners lucky enough to obtain a plant with an intact root system, and who take care to provide the strongly acid conditions and open drainage the species demands, often reap the reward of a large, floriferous colony after a few years. Indeed, *C. acaule* was once known as the "common" lady's slipper. It can form large stands where acidic conditions naturally prevail, possibly avoiding competition through its ability to tolerate acidic soils. Few other species find this environment satisfactory. While the orchid may depend in part upon the fungal symbiont for its nutrition in natural settings, successful cultivation has been reported by growers who make no special effort to establish or maintain a mycorrhizal association. Cultivation of laboratory-propagated seedlings of *C. acaule* produced the first blooming plants in 2000 (Durkee).

Mature *Cypripedium acaule* plants may also require fungal assistance if growing conditions deteriorate, but they may become less dependent when conditions improve. A long-term study (Gill 1996) of some six thousand individual lady's slippers in Maryland and Virginia found the orchid extremely well adapted to wait out periods of unlikely reproductive success, ready to take advantage of the situation when ecological conditions change. The twenty-year study noted that reproductive failure was common in typical years, with only small numbers of plants flowering in any given year, and only 5 percent of flowers setting seed. However, the annual survival rate was 98 percent, and the plants were regarded as "functionally immortal." During the 1990–1991 growing season, major ecological changes occurred. The tree canopy in the study area suffered extensive damage from an infestation of the gypsy moth. The moths' depredations on the leaves of the trees opened the canopy, admitting more sunlight to ground-level perennials, including the lady's slippers. This had a strongly positive effect on the orchids. Flowering increased a whopping 600 percent. In part because more flowers were produced, and in part because nearby plants attractive to pollinators also grew and bloomed more profusely, the orchids enjoyed a nearly 800 percent increase in successful pollination and subsequent seed production. These observations support the notion that the orchid thrives in relatively open, sunny sites but suffers as the canopy grows over it. When fire or insect damage create an opening, allowing more sunlight in, the orchids respond with increased flowering and produce millions of seeds.

Mycorrhizal associations may play a role in supporting the nutritional needs of *Cypripedium acaule* during periods of minimal sun exposure and a consequently lowered rate of photosynthesis, even if these conditions persist for decades. Mycorrhizal associations would therefore be essential for the plant's survival in the wild. Cultivated plants, on the other hand, receive their nutrition at the hands of the gardener and thus need no fungal partner. This hypothesis has important implications for any attempt at reestablishment of this orchid on natural sites. Ironically, relocated plants might survive better under cultivation than in the wild, unless the proposed relocation site already supports a population of lady's slippers.

Other species of *Cypripedium*, as well as the other genera mentioned in this book, can be cultivated under artificial conditions. Many adapt well to pot culture in sterile media, besides growing well in the garden. To suggest that in each case of success the fungus is present, whereas in cases of failure it is not, merely begs the question. If cultural conditions are conducive to the growth and flowering of the orchid, it matters little if this were indirectly the result of successfully growing the fungal symbiont. By definition the two are found in the same natural environment, and cultural conditions should be the same for either organism.

89

Paul Christian (2003) of Paul Christian Rare Plants in the United Kingdom shares my doubts about a fungal requirement for terrestrial orchids in the garden. He points out that the orchid and the fungus do not "want" to aid each other's growth. Rather, the relationship is more a battle fought to a stalemate.

Having a nonobligatory (biologists would say "facultative") relationship with a fungal partner might offer distinct advantages to an orchid growing in a woodland dale. Orchids often colonize disturbed areas, taking advantage of clearings created by fallen trees, for example. In the hardwood coves of the southern Appalachians, an ancient tulip poplar can reach 10 feet in diameter and 100 feet in height before its inevitable demise. When a strong wind roars up the valley, bringing down one of these elderly giants, a considerable area is opened to the sunlight. Orchid seedlings may germinate and grow in the thick carpet of forest litter, the microclimate cooled and humidified by the dense forest surrounding them, basking in the sun for many years before shade returns. The forest never remains the same. A squirrel carries an acorn into the clearing, then drops it when startled by the approach of a fox. A cardinal leaves behind a dogwood seed from a berry he recently ate, fiery red like his plumage. As tree seedlings sprout and grow in the clearing, a new canopy begins to close over the orchid. It may grow thus in deepening shade for many years, increasingly relying on nutrients supplied by the fungus. Indifferent to light and darkness, the fungus, lacking chlorophyll, digests the humus surrounding the orchid's roots and in turn surrenders up some of the nutrients as the orchid digests its hyphae (Gill 1996).

Orchids may persist this way for many years. Gullible humans, on finding a colony in the damp under a hemlock tree, may assume they need more shade and water than they really do. Or, because the orchids are terrestrial, we may try to grow them in loam too heavy with clay or too waterlogged with peat, not realizing that they are, first and foremost, orchids, with thick, fleshy, delicate, absorbent roots in need of the right balance of water and air, just like their tropical cousins.

To be sure, some terrestrial orchids have taken the relationship with their fungal symbionts much farther than the facultative stage. Rather than relying on the fungus only when environmental conditions are less than optimal, some orchids have become totally dependent. However, they have also lost the ability to carry out photosynthesis and cannot manufacture food for themselves. The North American genus *Corallorhiza* is a typical example. In contrast to plants that carry out photosynthesis, *Corallorhiza* is finicky about the fungus with which it associates (Taylor and Bruns 1999).

While three species of fungi were found to be associated with one species of *Corallorhiza* and twenty were found with another, the two orchids had no fungi in common, even when they were growing together at the same site, suggesting that each species was controlling its acquisition of fungal associates. All of the fungi, however, were in the same family, one known for its participation in mycorrhizal associa-

Corallorhiza maculata. Photo by Philip Keenan.

Corallorhiza striata. Photo by Philip Keenan.

tions. Since different fungi were found in association with the same species of *Corallorhiza* in different microhabitats, it appears that the orchid makes do with the locally available members of a restricted group of fungal species. *Corallorhiza* and the similarly nonphotosynthetic *Hexalectris* are thus unlikely to be amenable to cultivation outside the natural habitat unless provided with an appropriate fungus. While either genus has its charm, neither bears sufficiently showy flowers to merit the trouble of cultivation.

Mature photosynthetic orchids, including all the horticulturally desirable, showy species, can grow independently of fungal symbionts in the garden or greenhouse. This statement makes sense logically and has been empirically demonstrated many times (see, for example, Durkee 2000). The notion that successful cultivation of terrestrial orchids necessarily involves a fungal symbiont should be discarded. On the other hand, mycorrhizae deliberately introduced into the medium can play a valuable role in the propagation of orchids from seed (Zettler 1996). Mycorrhizae may thus be considered helpful, but not necessary, to the cultivation of hardy terrestrial orchids.

Hardy Orchids
Through the Seasons

THE ENDLESS CYCLE OF THE SEASONS, SO CLEARLY MARKED by the ebb and flow of blooms in the Tennessee Valley and its defining highlands to the east and west, calls forth from every garden its most precious element: change. Properly handled in the garden design, seasonal change contributes to the sense of place native gardens can so effectively evoke. Hardy orchids add their special notes to every movement of the seasonal symphony. They have adapted their growth cycles not only to include the obligatory dormant stage but also to vary their times of bloom and pod (fruit) development to maximize their chances of pollination and seed production. Thus, we can have them in bloom, or at least in active growth, nearly every month.

Spring

By the time the weather warms and such garden favorites as bluebells and irises bloom, the various cypripediums send up flowers, with the irresistible pink lady's slipper (*Cypripedium acaule*) usually appearing

93

first. Though exacting in its cultural requirements, this species need not be ruled out for a specimen planting.

Among the fifty-two species of orchids native to the eastern United States, surely *Cypripedium acaule* receives the most attention. Long the subject of botanical mystery and horticultural myth, this remarkable plant grows throughout eastern North America, from northern Georgia and Alabama to Newfoundland and Alberta. The commonest and most widespread member of its genus (Cribb 1997), notably absent from the federal list of endangered species, *C. acaule* often forms spectacular stands on sites that fulfill its peculiar ecological needs. Horticulturists fail to understand this orchid perhaps with more regularity than any other wildflower in North America. It does demand rather precise cultural conditions, but its supposed requirement for a symbiotic root fungus remains the most commonly cited explanation for how difficult it is to establish. As previously mentioned, botanists recognize the existence of mycorrhizal associations in a majority of vascular plants, many of which, of course, have been cultivated for centuries. In this regard, the pink lady's slipper is no different from thousands of other plants with precise cultural needs. Some gardeners have been growing this species successfully for decades. In fact, a British gardening magazine featured the orchid in 1792 (Cribb and Bailes 1989).

The extraordinary extent to which pink lady's slippers are dependent upon fungal symbionts in the wild may have led to the incorrect assumption that the symbiosis is also essential to their cultivation. As with all orchids, *Cypripedium acaule* depends upon establishing a mycorrhizal association for its seedling development. If the germinating orchid makes contact with a fungal partner of an appropriate type, fungal filaments invade the seedling, substituting for an extensive root system that the seedling has not yet developed, and providing carbohydrates that the orchid cannot yet produce via photosynthesis. Seedlings that fail to establish this association die, while successful seedlings slowly grow as a protocorm nourished by the fungus. *Cypripedium acaule* seedlings may remain in the protocorm stage for several years before developing a green leaf. However, once the plant becomes ca-

A trio of container-grown *Cypripedium acaule*.

pable of photosynthesis, it has no further need for the symbiont, as long as growing conditions remain suitable (Durkee 2000).

I have successfully cultivated several specimens of *Cypripedium acaule* since 1998. The oldest one flowered for the first time on 18 April 2001. This plant and eight other individuals of varying size grew for several years in a plastic nursery container (18 inches in diameter and 15 inches deep, or about 16 gallons) sunk into the ground in a spot shaded by deciduous trees. A bottom layer of 4 inches of gritty silica sand (of the type used for sandblasting) provided drainage. The growing mix consisted of two parts composted pine bark fines, one part coarse sand, and one part long-fiber sphagnum moss. Mulched in fall with a mixture of cypress bark chips, pine bark and cone chips, and pine needles, they weathered a total of five winters before being relocated.

Irrigation is generally not needed, except during an unusually dry period, when the pink lady's slipper grows outdoors. The plants easily weather sporadic summer dry spells. The growing mix must never become waterlogged, which will impede aeration and result in rotting of the roots. Cool, overly wet conditions may also result in crown rot. This situation typically occurs in spring. To avoid the problem, remove winter mulch as soon as the growing tips break dormancy. If your area experiences late cold snaps after the weather has begun to warm up, have a supply of last year's pine needles available to cover the plants should the need arise.

Maintaining strongly acidic, nutrient-poor conditions in the growing medium is essential to the horticulture of *Cypripedium acaule* (Durkee 2000). Seedlings adapt to a range of pH in the laboratory, so it is possible that the adaptation to growing in strongly acidic soil benefits the plant largely because many potentially competing species cannot grow in soil that offers such low levels of nutrients. Poor nutrient availability results from comparatively little soil microbial activity, in contrast to soils with a pH closer to neutral. Because of the adaptation to infertile soil, *C. acaule* may be damaged or killed by the application of fertilizer. Gardeners are likely to be familiar with other plants that do not perform well when grown in overly rich conditions. Nasturtiums, for

Cypripedium acaule, three years after purchase at a DIY store.

example, usually respond to fertilization with a profusion of leafy growth and few blooms, but the pink lady's slipper presents an extreme example, yellowing and wilting with astonishing rapidity. Media components such as moss and pine bark help create an acidic growing environment. Acidifying the water used for irrigation by adding ordinary white vinegar at the rate of 1 ounce per gallon yields a solution with a pH of about 4.5. Only rainwater, demineralized tap water, or distilled water should be used for irrigation, although an occasional dousing with hard water does not appear to harm plants.

As one might expect, the pink lady's slipper may seem rare because it occurs only where the extreme habitat type it requires can be found.

A natural stand of *Cypripedium acaule* in Knox County, Tennessee.

In the Tennessee Valley, it frequently colonizes sites dominated by second-growth coniferous trees. Once established, a population may persist for decades, taking advantage of an occasional opening in the forest canopy, producing large numbers of offspring during the comparatively brief interval until the forest regrows.

The remarkable flower of the pink lady's slipper functions as a bumblebee trap. The flower's characteristic pouchlike lip is incurved from either side, forming a trap door admitting any insect heavy enough to fall through. Usually the victim is a bumblebee. Because the "door" only opens inward, the insect is forced to exit through a tunnel at the back of the flower. In so doing, the insect's thorax acquires the orchid's sticky pollinia. If the bee has by chance been entrapped previously, the pollinia it carries are scraped off on the stigma, strategically positioned near the entrance to the tunnel. Interestingly, the orchid offers no nectar reward to its pollinators, apparently relying upon deception alone.

Perhaps the most intriguing aspect of the pink lady's slipper is its potential medicinal value. Like several other North American cypripediums, the rhizomes contain glycosides and other components higher in molecular weight that confer a sedative or antispasmodic effect on preparations made from them. The Cherokees have used it as a vermifuge for centuries. Although an overdose can result in hallucinations, properly administered, cypripedium extracts produce "the relaxing capabilities of opium without the side effects" (Cribb 1997). Given that this effect has been known to western science since at least 1828 (Rafinesque), it is perhaps not too bold to suggest that the subject deserves further investigation by modern pharmacological methods.

Propagated *Cypripedium acaule* plants are available by mail order, as are legally salvaged wild specimens. (See "Suppliers and Organizations.") If provided with a loose, fluffy, freely draining growing medium at a pH of 4–5, the pink lady's slipper can be successfully cultivated. The availability of laboratory-propagated seedlings and nursery-grown mature plants means that any gardener willing to expend a little extra effort can enjoy the pink lady's slipper as it sends up its lovely, intricate flowers each spring.

Summer

Summer heat seems to call for warm, even hot, colors in the garden. Orange fringed orchid (*Platanthera ciliaris*) complies by producing a dense cluster of perfectly citrus-orange florets, no two exactly alike. It favors moist, sunny, open spaces and attracts both hummingbirds and butterflies with its bold, upright growth. Like most fringed orchids, it thrives in a bog garden.

Sending up its flower cluster nearly a meter, the orange fringed orchid glows like a candle against the dark green of its frequent partner, running cedar. Not a cedar at all but a club moss in the genus *Lycopodium*, running cedar carpets the ground in acid woods. Mountain folk gathered its evergreen foliage for Christmas decorations. Visit a sunny patch in a stand of pines or oaks with running cedar twining through the leaf litter, and chances are, if it's August, the orange fringed orchid will be in bloom. The complex flower structure, fringed florets, and coloration make it unmistakable. The color of individuals varies somewhat on both the yellow and red sides of orange, but always invokes the citrus fruit.

Orange fringed orchid pretty much defines "bog orchid" for horticultural purposes. It grows well in an artificial bog, in slightly acidic media, in full sun. If it receives weak monthly fertilization from its emergence in spring until flowering begins, it grows vigorously and develops one or at most two lateral growth buds that can eventually be detached to produce more plants. Annoyingly, its reproductive rate lags far behind that of many others of its genus, which can double the numbers of blooming-size plants in a clump within only two or three years.

What it lacks in prolificacy, though, this orchid makes up for in garden presence, attracting butterflies and hummingbirds to its numerous nectaries and generally calling attention to itself. It partners well with other orchids having similar needs, and with companion plants such as Barbara's buttons (*Marshallia grandiflora*). Growing it with running cedar, however, poses a challenge, as the *Lycopodium* does not take kindly to captivity and probably should best remain (running free, as it were) along the forest floor.

Platanthera ciliaris, close-up of flower spike.

Fall

With the first hints of fall, and often before the end of summer, fragrant nodding lady's tresses (*Spiranthes cernua* var. *odorata* 'Chadd's Ford') develops bloom spikes that remain until the first frost kills them. In my zone 7 garden, this can mean blooms into November. Because this almost rampantly growing moisture lover makes an excellent cut flower, the bloom spikes can be rescued and brought indoors when bad weather threatens. In a vase of water with floral preservative they last more than a week, their vanilla fragrance a pleasant reminder of the warmer days recently relinquished.

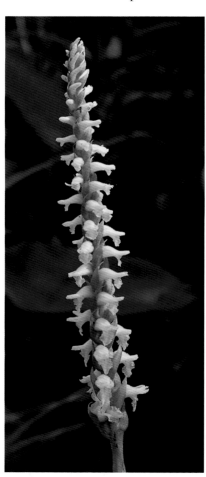

Spiranthes cernua var. *odorata* 'Chadd's Ford' blooms in my bog garden.

Each time a generalization is made about the orchid family, exceptions crop up to make life more interesting. An exception to the rule that orchids dislike wet feet, fragrant nodding lady's tresses offers exceptional garden value. Wide-ranging along America's eastern coastal plain and in spotty locations elsewhere, this native orchid was among the first to hold the distinction of having a named cultivar introduced into the nursery trade. Barry Glick (1995), authority on rare plants and owner of Sunshine Farm and Gardens in Renick, West Virginia, has sung its praises.

Found growing in a ditch near Bear, Delaware, in the 1960s, *Spiranthes cernua* var. *odorata* 'Chadd's Ford' received a Certificate of Cultural Merit from the American Orchid Society in 1973. The awarded plant was a division of the original discovery and was grown by Merlin Brubaker. The cultivar name, 'Chadd's Ford', commemorates Brubaker's hometown in Pennsylvania. 'Chadd's Ford' enjoys several distinctions that set it apart from the rank and file of its species. More robust, with larger and more numerous flowers, the plant exudes a rich vanilla fragrance. Given a fertile, moist environment with full sun, it forms large clumps quickly by sending out runners that bear new plants at their tips.

The dozen plants I obtained from Barry Glick in 2000 have multiplied to more than fifty individuals. By observing several pot-grown plants, I determined that each healthy individual produces an average of five offspring per growing season, a reproductive rate comparable to that of numerous garden perennials.

A propensity for adapting to varied culture conditions makes *Spiranthes cernua* var. *odorata* 'Chadd's Ford' among the more rewarding and desirable native orchids for the outdoor garden.

Winter

Even during the gloomy, brief, and usually wet days of winter, cranefly orchid (*Tipularia discolor*) soldiers on, taking advantage of the bouts of winter sun reaching it once the tree canopy falls. Without competition from the other forest species, now dormant, it stores food and undergoes developmental changes that will permit bloom later in the year, during summer, when pollinators venture out and about. As days

shorten and temperatures cool, the unusual little cranefly orchid emerges from the leaf litter, usually in acidic, deciduous woods, its single spade-shaped leaf often easy to spot but overlooked on the forest floor. The genus name, *Tipularia*, remarks upon the resemblance of the flower spike to a hovering cluster of small craneflies, members of the entomological family Tipularidae. The species epithet, *discolor*, reflects the two-colored winter leaf, usually a dark olive on the upper surface and a rich claret beneath.

Tipularia discolor in winter leaf.

Cranefly orchid shares with a few other species the survival strategy of growing during winter. By spring the winter leaf has shriveled and disappeared. The flower spike appears, as if by magic, later in the season in the shade of the woods.

Although not remarkable in the horticultural sense, cranefly orchid owns a place in my garden because of its inverted life cycle. Although numerous European species are similarly summer-dormant, I have not yet attempted to grow any of them, as our sometimes bitter winter weather requires that they be coddled in an alpine greenhouse.

Having experimented with about fifty plants removed from the pink lady's slipper salvage site described in chapter 1, I have learned that *Tipularia*, weathering cold, drying winter winds with impunity, grows best in the "driest" area of my bog bed, where the medium remains slightly moist, is well shaded in summer, and has dappled sun in winter—in other words, under a large deciduous tree. It prefers a strongly acid growing medium and consequently little or no added fertilizer. Cultural methodology similar to that employed for *Cypripedium acaule*, differing only in the moisture level of the medium, has given the best results.

Bletilla: The Ideal Beginner's Plant

My first real success with hardy orchids came many years ago when, lured by the blurb in a mail-order catalog, I purchased six corms of Chinese ground orchids (*Bletilla striata*). I gave them a choice spot in the foundation bed I had constructed on the northeast side of my house. Dubbed my "biodiversity bed," this growing area showcased the best of my plant collection. Eventually, more than fifty woodland plants established themselves in this bed, including wildflowers from Vasey's trillium (*Trillium vaseyi*) to goldenseal (*Hydrastis canadensis*), ferns, hostas, and a splendid cutleaf Japanese maple. The orchids stole the show the second spring after their fall transplanting and continued to do so every year until 2003, increasing in number and beauty. During the spring of 2003 they were transplanted to my new house and divided, yielding more than one hundred plants. In beds more carefully designed with their wishes in mind, these plants can be counted on for color, pleasing form, and fragrance, for as many Mays as I expect to see, and then some.

Employing only a modest amount of horticultural knowledge, I had constructed that first biodiversity bed with good drainage and a high-quality organic growing mix that contained compost, leaves, peat moss, composted pine bark, and the heavy clay topsoil that thinly covered the yard. To this I added blood and bone meal, following the recommendations on the bags. I reasoned that my best plants deserved the best soil, so I used the same growing medium I had been using in my vegetable garden. After the plants were established for a full growth cycle, the bed required only occasional irrigation. The northeastern exposure proved itself the perfect combination of sun and shade for the orchids.

I have often wondered why more orchid fanciers, not to mention outdoor gardeners, don't grow *Bletilla*. Its ease of culture may deter orchidists who practice a bizarre form of snobbery, favoring challenging species over more readily rewarding ones. The backyard gardeners may hesitate simply because it's an orchid. It should, however, enjoy a place of honor in anyone's plant collection. Given the right amount of exposure (more sun in the North, as usual, and more shade in the South), *Bletilla* adapts as readily to the shaded perennial border as do a hundred other garden plants. Wet feet will rot its roots and corms, and sometimes a late cold snap will produce unsightly leaf tip damage, but otherwise season after season passes without incident as each clump blissfully increases in size and floral exuberance. Typical garden pests—including, wonder of wonders, snails and slugs—leave it alone. Insects appear to visit only to pollinate the sweet-smelling flowers with their ruffled rose and magenta lips.

About ten years after the first plants arrived, I added a dozen corms of two interesting white variants of *Bletilla striata*. *Bletilla striata* var. *alba* bears pure white flowers with a pale pink blush. Smaller and slower growing than the wild type, though equally friendly to the gardener, it never quite reaches the same height, forming a second tier of blooms in mixed plantings. Somewhat less frequently seen, though in all respects identical to *B. striata* var. *alba*, is a form with variegated leaves called 'First Kiss'. It blooms alongside the other types, the parallel venation of its leaves enhanced by the white striping.

A few years ago, *Bletilla ochracea* was offered by a large mail-order

Bletilla striata grows at the base of a Japanese maple.

nursery, and I ordered six corms. They bloomed well the first season, about a week after *B. striata* flowers began to open, their yellow coloration harmonizing splendidly with the other *Bletilla* plants in the same bed. *Bletilla ochracea* plants grow about a foot tall, about half the maximum height of either of the *B. striata* types. In my experience they grow just like their cousins, though unfortunately they do not increase as rapidly. My plants were moved during the spring of 2003 along with the rest of my collection. I planted them in a deep bed constructed of treated pine, in a prepared growing mix.

Growth rate, plant size, and floriferousness increase in *Bletilla* with fertilization. Soluble chemical orchid fertilizer at one-half the manufacturer's recommended dilution applied monthly during the growing season supplements annual amendments of blood and bone meal applied in late winter. Timed-release fertilizers such as Osmocote have also worked well in small beds and pots.

Bletilla needs plenty of rain as the weather warms up and through the blooming season, but the need to avoid water standing around the roots cannot be overemphasized. Well-drained beds, ideally raised slightly above grade, will give the best results and encourage the roots to spread, in turn promoting new growth that may later be divided. By the time summer really turns up the heat, the plants become rather drought tolerant and need no more watering than, say, a bed of annuals such as marigolds or zinnias.

Ease of propagation is perhaps the most desirable horticultural feature of the *Bletilla* species (and, according to various authors, their hybrids). Mature clumps can be divided with a shovel and transplanted immediately, anytime after flowering. The more fastidious may choose to wait until the plants are dormant. Then the corms may be lifted with a garden fork. After removing the soil from around the roots, cut the corms with a sharp knife so that each piece has two or more growing points. The cut surfaces may be dusted with powdered sulfur, or simply set aside for a day or two to allow the wounds to dry. The prepared corms may then be replanted in the garden or stored under refrigeration in plastic bags of dry peat moss. Replant stored corms in spring, as soon as the ground can be worked.

Clark T. Riley (1999) describes *Bletilla* as growing from seed "with abandon." He goes on to say that "any of the popular media or even . . . dampened *Sphagnum* moss" give reliable germination, though at a lower rate on the moss. Further, he reports that seedlings may bloom only two or three years after their parents were pollinated.

Ease of culture and propagation, exciting prospects for hybridization both among the species and across generic lines with *Arundina* and *Calanthe*, and darn nice flowers and foliage should earn *Bletilla* a place in any garden. Perhaps we should change its common name to "queen of the hardy orchids."

7 A Catalog of Hardy and Half-Hardy Orchids

IN THIS CATALOG, RATHER THAN CREATE A NARRATIVE for each selected orchid species, something I find tediously repetitive in many other compendia, I list the essential cultivation information for each orchid, along with notable facts in the form of "comments." My intention is to enable gardeners to determine quickly and easily the suitability of any given species or hybrid according to their particular gardening needs and desires.

It should be noted that this catalog is neither exhaustive nor entirely based upon my own gardening experience. Plants in my collection will be so identified. Only references containing information about cultural requirements are included. For the sake of completeness, information about species already discussed is also given. All of the cultivation techniques referenced here are fully described in earlier chapters. Recipes for various orchid media, such as the Tullock general purpose mix, are listed in chapter 2.

When considering the season of bloom, variations in climate must be taken into account. As a rule, garden events occur about two weeks later as you move from a warmer zone to a colder one. Thus, it is difficult to give a specific month in which blooms may be expected. Local climate variations can be considerable. Parts of my yard are a full five degrees warmer than others, depending upon shelter from the house, sun exposure, and so forth. For predictive purposes, there is no substitute for keeping complete records of the events in your garden and evaluating them in terms of the local weather:

EARLY SPRING	Around the frost date
SPRING	Two to four weeks after the frost date
SUMMER	After the ground is thoroughly warmed and all danger of frost is past (may be equally divided into early, mid, and late summer, until the leaves start to turn)
FALL	As leaves begin to change color, through the first frost
WINTER	Between the first frost of fall and the last frost of spring

Hardiness zones are inferred from the distribution pattern of the plant, or are published estimates of hardiness. The USDA compiles information about the average minimum temperatures throughout the country and maps climate zones across North America. Beginning with zone 10, where the average minimum temperature falls between 30°F and 40°F, each zone differs from the next by ten degrees. My garden lies approximately at the transition between zones 6 and 7, only rarely experiencing winter cold below −10°F. Plants said to be hardy over a range of zones can be expected to survive winter in the zone with the lower number. Some terrestrial orchids, such as bletillas, grow well without a winter cold period, requiring only drought to induce their dormancy. These species grow outdoors in North America all the way to zone 10. Other species, such as cypripediums, require a period of cold dormancy and may do poorly further south than the maximum recommended zone.

A USDA hardiness zone map is included at the back of the book, and others can be found on the Web. The American Horticulture Society is a good place to start: www.gardenweb.com. This site conveniently provides scalable maps for various parts of the world; click on a spot on a larger map to select a region for closer inspection. Orchidists interested in species from Europe will find maps for that continent and its regional subdivisions, with climatic zones corresponding to the USDA standard.

For orchid species listed in this catalog that are not native to the United States, hardiness zones are extrapolated from reported minimum temperatures at which these plants will survive, and are extended to zone 10, which would encompass most of southwestern Europe.

The American Horticultural Society has also established "heat zones" that take into account summer maximum temperatures. I have not attempted to translate the hardy orchid information to provide heat zone recommendations, but suffice it to say that species usually found where summers are cool often do poorly in the Sunbelt region of the United States, due to the oppressive summer heat. This may require, for example, that gardeners in the Southeast construct a cool greenhouse in order to flower some species.

Numerous factors, including sun exposure, elevation, nearby structures, and wind, can alter a given microhabitat (such as a raised flowerbed under your eastern eaves) by a full zone or more. Draw upon your experience with other plants in your garden, comparing your results to the recommendations found in books, seed catalogs, and so forth. Extrapolate this experience to selecting hardy orchids.

Anacamptis pyramidalis

Pyramidal orchid

NATIVE HABITAT Europe

SEASON OF BLOOM Summer

BLOOM COLOR Pink, sometimes white

HARDINESS Zones 7–10 (minimum temperature 25°F)

SITING & EXPOSURE Full sun

DRAINAGE Average

MEDIUM Tullock general purpose mix with lime

pH 7–8

IRRIGATION This plant requires constant moisture.

FERTILIZATION As for any perennial, light applications at the beginning and end of the growing season are likely to have the greatest impact.

MULCH Apply a 1-inch layer of any suitable material when the plants are dormant.

COMMERCIAL AVAILABILITY See "Suppliers and Organizations."

COMMENTS The evening fragrance is said to be similar to carnations. The common name comes from the pyramidal shape of the flower spike. This orchid sometimes appears in lawns, which should be an indicator of the conditions it prefers.

REFERENCES Beyrle 2003, Christian 2003, Cribb and Bailes 1989

Aplectrum hyemale

Puttyroot, Adam and Eve

NATIVE HABITAT Eastern North America

SEASON OF BLOOM Early spring

BLOOM COLOR Yellow-green or maroon-purple

HARDINESS Zones 3–8

SITING & EXPOSURE Summer shade, winter sun

DRAINAGE Average

MEDIUM Tullock general purpose mix or Phillips (1985) woodland wildflower mix

pH 5–6

Aplectrum hyemale, winter leaf.

IRRIGATION This plant is drought tolerant late in the season but needs ample moisture in winter and spring until the flowers fade.

FERTILIZATION Feed annually with organic amendments to the growing bed.

MULCH Apply a 1-inch layer of any suitable material after the winter leaf appears in fall.

COMMERCIAL AVAILABILITY See "Suppliers and Organizations."

COMMENTS This orchid is easily propagated from seed or by division of the rootstock of a large plant. Its common names derive from sticky sap contained within the tuber, and from the tuber's growth pattern. "Adam" is last year's tuber, from which "Eve," this year's tuber, springs forth. The plant produces a single, pleated leaf, blue-green and marked with silver veins, that dies down in early spring before the flower spike appears. *Aplectrum unguiculatum* is the Japanese counterpart. This plant has been in my collection for several years.

REFERENCES Bentley 2000, Cribb and Bailes 1989, Glick 1995

Arethusa bulbosa

Bog rose

NATIVE HABITAT From Newfoundland and Quebec south, rarely as far as the Southern Appalachians

SEASON OF BLOOM Summer

BLOOM COLOR Fuchsia with white markings on the lip

HARDINESS Zones 2–6

SITING & EXPOSURE Full sun

DRAINAGE Requires bog conditions

MEDIUM Tullock general purpose mix

pH 4.5–5.5

IRRIGATION This plant requires constant moisture.

FERTILIZATION Feed lightly with commercial orchid fertilizer during the growing season.

MULCH Apply a thin layer of grass clippings or chopped pine needles in fall.

COMMERCIAL AVAILABILITY This species is not available.

COMMENTS Considered difficult to cultivate, the bog rose prefers cool temperatures and is likely to fail where summers are hot. Plants have been raised from seed to flower on sterile media.

REFERENCES Cribb and Bailes 1989, Yanetti 1996

Bletilla **Brigantes** (*B. striata* × *B. ochracea*)

Brigantes

NATIVE HABITAT Of hybrid origin, 1994

SEASON OF BLOOM Spring

BLOOM COLOR Variable, combinations of purple and yellow

HARDINESS Unknown

SITING & EXPOSURE Full sun to partial shade

DRAINAGE Average

MEDIUM Phillips (1985) woodland wildflower mix or any reasonable garden soil

pH 5–7

IRRIGATION This plant is drought tolerant late in the season but needs ample moisture in spring and early summer until the flowers fade.

FERTILIZATION Incorporate organic amendments each fall, or feed monthly from emergence to blooming with half-strength commercial orchid fertilizer.

MULCH Apply 1–2 inches of any mulch material after the leaves die back in fall. The plants may need extra protection in early spring to avoid stem tip damage from late frosts.

COMMERCIAL AVAILABILITY See "Suppliers and Organizations."

COMMENTS Brigantes is similar to its parents in terms of culture. Although not commonly available, this hybrid is worth seeking out. It is vigorous, with floral characteristics intermediate between the parents.

REFERENCES Christian 2003, Fraser and Fraser 2003, Riley 1999

Bletilla ochracea

Yellow Chinese ground orchid

NATIVE HABITAT China

SEASON OF BLOOM Spring

BLOOM COLOR Yellow with red dots

HARDINESS Zones 6–10 (zone 5 with protection)

SITING & EXPOSURE Full sun to partial shade

DRAINAGE Average

MEDIUM Phillips (1985) woodland wildflower mix or any reasonable garden soil

pH 5–7

IRRIGATION This plant is drought tolerant late in the season but needs ample moisture in spring and early summer until the flowers fade.

Bletilla ochracea.

FERTILIZATION Incorporate organic amendments each fall, or feed monthly from emergence to blooming with half-strength commercial orchid fertilizer.

MULCH Apply 1–2 inches of any mulch material after the leaves die back in fall. The plants may need extra protection in early spring to avoid stem tip damage from late frosts.

COMMERCIAL AVAILABILITY This species is not commonly available in the trade, but see "Suppliers and Organizations."

COMMENTS Smaller than *B. striata*, this species blooms about two weeks later in my garden and grows less vigorously. Otherwise it appears to be bulletproof.

REFERENCES Cribb and Bailes 1989, Fraser and Fraser 2003, Riley 1999

Bletilla striata

Chinese ground orchid, hardy Chinese orchid

NATIVE HABITAT China and Japan

SEASON OF BLOOM Spring

BLOOM COLOR Bright purple, pale pink, or white

HARDINESS Zones 5–10

SITING & EXPOSURE Full sun to partial shade

DRAINAGE Average

MEDIUM Phillips (1985) woodland wildflower mix or any reasonable garden soil

pH 5–7

IRRIGATION This plant is drought tolerant late in the season but needs ample moisture in spring and early summer until the flowers fade.

FERTILIZATION Incorporate organic amendments each fall, or feed monthly from emergence to blooming with half-strength commercial orchid fertilizer.

MULCH Apply 1–2 inches of any mulch material after the leaves die back in fall. The plants may need extra protection in early spring to avoid stem tip damage from late frosts.

COMMERCIAL AVAILABILITY See "Suppliers and Organizations."

COMMENTS This is one of the more easily grown and rewarding species at home in a shady perennial bed or woodland garden.

REFERENCES Christian 2003, Cribb and Bailes 1989, Fraser and Fraser 2003, Riley 1999

Bletilla striata var. *alba*

White Chinese ground orchid

NATIVE HABITAT China and Japan

SEASON OF BLOOM Spring

BLOOM COLOR White, often with a pale pink blush

HARDINESS Zones 5–10

SITING & EXPOSURE Full sun to partial shade

DRAINAGE Average

MEDIUM Phillips (1985) woodland wildflower mix or any reasonable garden soil

pH 5–7

IRRIGATION This plant is drought tolerant late in the season but needs ample moisture in spring and early summer until the flowers fade.

Bletilla striata.

Bletilla striata var. *alba.*

FERTILIZATION Incorporate organic amendments each fall, or feed monthly from emergence to blooming with half-strength commercial orchid fertilizer.

MULCH Apply 1–2 inches of any mulch material after the leaves die back in fall. The plants may need extra protection in early spring to avoid stem tip damage from late frosts.

COMMERCIAL AVAILABILITY See "Suppliers and Organizations."

COMMENTS Less robust and slower growing than the wild type of *B. striata*, this variety is otherwise of similar hardiness and culture. A form with leaves variegated in white stripes is occasionally available and worth seeking out. *Bletilla striata* var. *alba* and *B. striata* have provided enjoyment in my garden for decades. Both make excellent cut flowers, the peak bloom time usually coinciding with Memorial Day celebrations.

REFERENCES Christian 2003, Cribb and Bailes 1989, Fraser and Fraser 2003, Riley 1999

Bletilla Yokohama (*Bletilla striata* × *B. formosana*)

Yokohama

NATIVE HABITAT Of hybrid origin, 1956

SEASON OF BLOOM Spring

Bletilla Yokohama. Photo by Dick Cavender.

BLOOM COLOR Bright purple

HARDINESS Unknown but probably at least to zone 8

SITING & EXPOSURE Full sun to partial shade

DRAINAGE Average

MEDIUM Phillips (1985) woodland wildflower mix or any reasonable garden soil

pH 5–7

IRRIGATION This plant is drought tolerant late in the season but needs ample moisture in spring and early summer until the flowers fade.

FERTILIZATION Incorporate organic amendments each fall, or feed monthly from emergence to blooming with half-strength commercial orchid fertilizer.

MULCH Apply 1–2 inches of any mulch material after the leaves die back in fall. The plants may need extra protection in early spring to avoid stem tip damage from late frosts.

COMMERCIAL AVAILABILITY See "Suppliers and Organizations."

COMMENTS Yokohama is taller than *B. striata* but may not be as hardy, as *B. formosana* is not reliably so.

REFERENCES Fraser and Fraser 2003, Riley 1999

Caladenia caerulea

Blue spider orchid

NATIVE HABITAT Australia

SEASON OF BLOOM Winter (summer-dormant)

BLOOM COLOR Blue

HARDINESS Zone 10 (minimum temperature 39°F)

SITING & EXPOSURE Partial shade

DRAINAGE Sharp drainage inferred from preference for sandy soils

MEDIUM Terrestrial mix with wood chips, or eucalyptus shavings

pH 5–6

IRRIGATION Plants should be kept moist during active growth and dry during dormancy.

FERTILIZATION Incorporate organic amendments only, as natural habitat is likely to be low in nutrient availability.

MULCH Apply 1–2 inches of any mulch material after the leaves die back.

COMMERCIAL AVAILABILITY See "Suppliers and Organizations."

COMMENTS Members of this genus are difficult to cultivate. *Caladenia caerulea* is found in sandy soils in coastal regions. It blooms during dormancy and should not be repotted until after the blooms fade.

REFERENCES Beyrle 2003, Cribb and Bailes 1989, Pridgeon 1992

Caladenia carnea

Pink spider orchid

NATIVE HABITAT Eastern Australia

SEASON OF BLOOM Winter (summer-dormant)

BLOOM COLOR Pink

HARDINESS Zone 10 (minimum temperature 39°F)

SITING & EXPOSURE Partial shade
DRAINAGE Sharp drainage inferred from preference for sandy soils
MEDIUM Terrestrial mix with wood chips, or eucalyptus shavings
pH 5–6
IRRIGATION Plants should be kept moist during active growth and dry during dormancy.
FERTILIZATION Incorporate organic amendments only, as natural habitat is likely to be low in nutrient availability.
MULCH Apply 1–2 inches of any mulch material after the leaves die back.
COMMERCIAL AVAILABILITY See "Suppliers and Organizations."
COMMENTS The flowers, which appear at the end of the spring growth phase, sometimes produce a musky odor.
REFERENCES Beyrle 2003, Cribb and Bailes 1989, Pridgeon 1992

Caladenia discoidea

Bee spider orchid
NATIVE HABITAT Western Australia
SEASON OF BLOOM Winter (summer-dormant)
BLOOM COLOR Greenish with purple markings
HARDINESS Zone 10 (minimum temperature 39°F)
SITING & EXPOSURE Partial shade
DRAINAGE Sharp drainage inferred from preference for sandy soils
MEDIUM Terrestrial mix with wood chips, or eucalyptus shavings
pH 5–6
IRRIGATION Plants should be kept moist during active growth and dry during dormancy.
FERTILIZATION Incorporate organic amendments only, as natural habitat is likely to be low in nutrient availability.
MULCH Apply 1–2 inches of any mulch material after the leaves die back.
COMMERCIAL AVAILABILITY See "Suppliers and Organizations."
COMMENTS Keep this species moist. After blooms fade, dry off and repot.
REFERENCES Beyrle 2003, Cribb and Bailes 1989, Pridgeon 1992

Caladenia eminens

White spider orchid
NATIVE HABITAT Western Australia
SEASON OF BLOOM Winter (summer-dormant)

BLOOM COLOR White

HARDINESS Zone 10 (minimum temperature 39°F)

SITING & EXPOSURE Partial shade

DRAINAGE Sharp drainage inferred from preference for sandy soils

MEDIUM Terrestrial mix with wood chips, or eucalyptus shavings

pH 5–6

IRRIGATION Plants should be kept moist during active growth and dry during dormancy.

FERTILIZATION Incorporate organic amendments only, as natural habitat is likely to be low in nutrient availability.

MULCH Apply 1–2 inches of any mulch material after the leaves die back.

COMMERCIAL AVAILABILITY See "Suppliers and Organizations."

COMMENTS This robust, deep-rooted species requires ample accommodations.

REFERENCES Beyrle 2003, Cribb and Bailes 1989, Pridgeon 1992

Calanthe alpina

NATIVE HABITAT China, Taiwan, and Japan

SEASON OF BLOOM Spring to summer

BLOOM COLOR Lilac with an orange lip

HARDINESS Zone 10 (minimum temperature 38°F)

SITING & EXPOSURE Alpine greenhouse (partial shade, with protection from wind damage)

DRAINAGE Sharp

MEDIUM Tropical orchid compost with added peat (50 percent bark, 30 percent peat, 20 percent pumice or perlite)

pH 5–6

IRRIGATION Plants should be kept barely moist, with leaves free of moisture.

FERTILIZATION Feed once or twice monthly with commercial orchid fertilizer.

MULCH No mulching is necessary.

COMMERCIAL AVAILABILITY See "Suppliers and Organizations."

COMMENTS *Calanthe* is a large genus of more than two hundred species, all well suited for the alpine greenhouse, and including species worth trying in a sheltered location in mild winter areas. *Calanthe alpina* endures hot summers and cold winters with snow cover and may grow even farther north than indicated. Many *Calanthe* hybrids exist; those involving any of the hardy species may also have potential in North America. This genus is so popular in Japan, it has its own society.

REFERENCES Cribb and Bailes 1989

Calanthe aristulifera

NATIVE HABITAT Japan

SEASON OF BLOOM Spring

BLOOM COLOR Lilac

HARDINESS Zone 10 (minimum temperature 38°F)

SITING & EXPOSURE Alpine greenhouse (partial shade, with protection from wind damage)

DRAINAGE Sharp

MEDIUM Tropical orchid compost with added peat (50 percent bark, 30 percent peat, 20 percent pumice or perlite)

pH 5–6

IRRIGATION Plants should be kept barely moist, with leaves free of moisture.

FERTILIZATION Feed once or twice monthly with commercial orchid fertilizer.

MULCH No mulching is necessary.

COMMERCIAL AVAILABILITY See "Suppliers and Organizations."

COMMENTS This species requires mild conditions. Natural hybrids with *C. discolor* and *C. striata* have been identified; these are considered more easily grown than the species.

REFERENCES Cribb and Bailes 1989

Calanthe discolor

NATIVE HABITAT China, Taiwan, and Japan

SEASON OF BLOOM Spring to summer

BLOOM COLOR Lilac

HARDINESS Zone 10 (minimum temperature 38°F)

SITING & EXPOSURE Alpine greenhouse (partial shade, with protection from wind damage)

DRAINAGE Sharp

MEDIUM Tropical orchid compost with added peat (50 percent bark, 30 percent peat, 20 percent pumice or perlite)

pH 5–6

IRRIGATION Plants should be kept barely moist, with leaves free of moisture.

FERTILIZATION Feed once or twice monthly with commercial orchid fertilizer.

MULCH Apply an annual mulch of leaf mold.

COMMERCIAL AVAILABILITY See "Suppliers and Organizations."

COMMENTS This species could be tried outdoors in mild climates.

REFERENCES Cribb and Bailes 1989

Calanthe izu-insularis

NATIVE HABITAT Izu Islands (Japan)

SEASON OF BLOOM Spring to summer

BLOOM COLOR Lilac

HARDINESS Zone 10 (minimum temperature 38°F)

SITING & EXPOSURE Alpine greenhouse (partial shade, with protection from wind damage)

DRAINAGE Sharp

MEDIUM Tropical orchid compost with added peat (50 percent bark, 30 percent peat, 20 percent pumice or perlite)

pH 5–6

IRRIGATION Plants should be kept barely moist, with leaves free of moisture.

FERTILIZATION Feed once or twice monthly with commercial orchid fertilizer.

MULCH No mulching is necessary.

COMMERCIAL AVAILABILITY See "Suppliers and Organizations."

COMMENTS This species may be merely a regional variant of C. *discolor*, with which it hybridizes to produce C. 'Kozu', considered a popular and easy subject by Japanese orchidists.

REFERENCES Cribb and Bailes 1989

Calanthe longicalcarata

NATIVE HABITAT Ryukyu Islands (Japan)

SEASON OF BLOOM Spring to summer

BLOOM COLOR Lilac, sometimes white

HARDINESS Zone 10 (minimum temperature 38°F)

SITING & EXPOSURE Alpine greenhouse (partial shade, with protection from wind damage)

123

DRAINAGE Sharp

MEDIUM Tropical orchid compost with added peat (50 percent bark, 30 percent peat, 20 percent pumice or perlite)

pH 5–6

IRRIGATION Plants should be kept barely moist, with leaves free of moisture.

FERTILIZATION Feed once or twice monthly with commercial orchid fertilizer.

MULCH No mulching is necessary.

COMMERCIAL AVAILABILITY See "Suppliers and Organizations."

COMMENTS This *Calanthe* is seldom seen outside large collections.

REFERENCES Cribb and Bailes 1989

Calanthe nipponica

NATIVE HABITAT Japan

SEASON OF BLOOM Variable

BLOOM COLOR Green with a yellow or sometimes orange lip

HARDINESS Zone 10 (minimum temperature 38°F)

SITING & EXPOSURE Alpine greenhouse (partial shade, with protection from wind damage)

DRAINAGE Sharp

MEDIUM Tropical orchid compost with added peat (50 percent bark, 30 percent peat, 20 percent pumice or perlite)

pH 5–6

IRRIGATION Plants should be kept barely moist, with leaves free of moisture.

FERTILIZATION Feed once or twice monthly with commercial orchid fertilizer.

MULCH No mulching is necessary.

COMMERCIAL AVAILABILITY See "Suppliers and Organizations."

COMMENTS This diminutive species remains under a foot in height and is considered difficult.

REFERENCESREFERENCES Cribb and Bailes 1989

Calanthe reflexa

NATIVE HABITAT From the Himalayas to Japan

SEASON OF BLOOM Variable

BLOOM COLOR Lavender, rarely white

HARDINESS Zone 10 (minimum temperature 38°F)

SITING & EXPOSURE Alpine greenhouse (partial shade, with protection from wind damage)

DRAINAGE Sharp

MEDIUM Tropical orchid compost with added peat (50 percent bark, 30 percent peat, 20 percent pumice or perlite)

pH 5–6

IRRIGATION Plants should be kept barely moist, with leaves free of moisture.

FERTILIZATION Feed once or twice monthly with commercial orchid fertilizer.

MULCH No mulching is necessary.

COMMERCIAL AVAILABILITY See "Suppliers and Organizations."

COMMENTS This species is evergreen and needs no rest period. It is found in swampy, cool sites with abundant composted plant matter, at elevations up to 8200 feet. The hybrid with *C. discolor*, known as *C.* 'Tokane', is considered an easy subject by Japanese orchidists, who also appreciate the fragrance.

REFERENCES Cribb and Bailes 1989, Pridgeon 1992

Calanthe tricarinata

NATIVE HABITAT From the Himalayas to Japan

SEASON OF BLOOM Spring

BLOOM COLOR Green with a crimson lip

HARDINESS Zone 10 (minimum temperature 38°F)

SITING & EXPOSURE Alpine greenhouse (partial shade, with protection from wind damage)

DRAINAGE Sharp

MEDIUM Tropical orchid compost with added peat (50 percent bark, 30 percent peat, 20 percent pumice or perlite)

pH 5–6

IRRIGATION Plants should be kept barely moist, with leaves free of moisture.

FERTILIZATION Feed once or twice monthly with commercial orchid fertilizer.

MULCH Apply pine straw or another light mulch.

COMMERCIAL AVAILABILITY This species is available from many sources, including some of those listed in "Suppliers and Organizations."

Calanthe tricarinata. Photo by Manuel Aubron.

COMMENTS Growing at elevations up to 9840 feet, this species may well be hardy as far north as zone 7. It is found in damp, shady locations with plenty of leaf litter and decomposing plant matter.

REFERENCES Cribb and Bailes 1989

Calopogon tuberosus

Grass pink

NATIVE HABITAT From maritime Canada to Cuba

SEASON OF BLOOM Summer

BLOOM COLOR Pink

HARDINESS Zones 2–10

SITING & EXPOSURE Full sun

DRAINAGE Requires bog conditions

MEDIUM Tullock general purpose mix or Cribb and Bailes (1989) bog mix

pH 4–6

IRRIGATION This plant requires constant moisture.

FERTILIZATION Incorporate organic amendments each fall, or feed monthly from emergence to blooming with half-strength commercial orchid fertilizer.

MULCH Apply 1–2 inches of grass clippings or chopped pine needles after the leaves die back in fall. The plants may need extra protection in early spring to avoid damage from late frosts.

Calopogon tuberosus. Photo by Philip Keenan.

COMMERCIAL AVAILABILITY Both seedlings and corms are commercially available. See "Suppliers and Organizations."

COMMENTS *Calopogon* needs moisture even during dormancy. If this cannot be assured outdoors, lift the corms and store refrigerated for at least three months before replanting.

REFERENCES Fraser and Fraser 2003, Whitlow 2003

Calypso bulbosa

Calypso orchid

NATIVE HABITAT Two varieties exist in North America, and the species is circumboreal in coniferous forests. The eastern form, var. *americana*, grows in bogs, while the western form, var. *occidentalis*, prefers drier sites with more shade.

SEASON OF BLOOM Winter (summer-dormant)

BLOOM COLOR Pink and yellow

HARDINESS Zones 2–5

SITING & EXPOSURE Partial (var. *americana*) to full (var. *occidentalis*) shade

DRAINAGE The eastern variety requires bog conditions; the western variety needs a drier site and could be expected to perform well alongside *Cypripedium acaule*.

MEDIUM Decomposing wood (var. *americana*) or decomposed fir, pine, or spruce needles (var. *occidentalis*). Do not add peat to the growing medium.

pH 6–7 for var. *americana*, but habitat preferences suggest more acidic conditions for var. *occidentalis*

IRRIGATION This plant requires constant moisture.

FERTILIZATION For var. *americana*, incorporate organic amendments each fall, or feed monthly from emergence to blooming with half-strength commercial orchid fertilizer. It can be inferred from the preferred habitat of var. *occidentalis* that it grows in nutrient-poor conditions and may not need fertilization.

MULCH Apply 1–2 inches of chopped pine needles after the leaves die back in fall.

COMMERCIAL AVAILABILITY See "Suppliers and Organizations."

COMMENTS This is a rare and possibly ephemeral orchid in the wild,

Calypso bulbosa var. *americana*. Photo by Philip Keenan.

but propagated plants are sometimes available. *Calypso bulbosa* dislikes summer heat and is not for gardeners in warmer zones. It is generally considered a challenge to cultivate successfully.

REFERENCES Cribb and Bailes 1989, Fraser and Fraser 2003, Smith 1993

Cymbidium faberi

NATIVE HABITAT From Nepal to Taiwan
SEASON OF BLOOM Variable
BLOOM COLOR Green with purple markings on the lip
HARDINESS Zone 10 (minimum temperature 38°F)
SITING & EXPOSURE Partial sun
DRAINAGE Allow to dry out slightly before watering
MEDIUM Tropical orchid mix
pH 5–6
IRRIGATION This plant requires constant moisture during the growing season.
FERTILIZATION Fertilize weekly with half-strength commercial tropical orchid fertilizer from March to October. Do not fertilize from November to February.
MULCH No mulching is necessary.
COMMERCIAL AVAILABILITY The genus includes many commercially important species and hybrids.
COMMENTS Growing at elevations up to 9515 feet and widely cultivated in China and Japan, this cymbidium should be cultivated in an alpine greenhouse or outdoors in mild areas. Hybrids incorporating hardier species may share their hardiness. Large-flowered cymbidiums, of which this is an example, require chilling to about 54°F to initiate blooming.
REFERENCES Cribb and Bailes 1989, Pridgeon 1992

Cymbidium floribundum

NATIVE HABITAT From southwestern China to Taiwan
SEASON OF BLOOM Fall
BLOOM COLOR Purple with a white lip spotted in red that becomes redder as the flower ages
HARDINESS Zone 10 (minimum temperature 38°F)
SITING & EXPOSURE Partial sun
DRAINAGE Allow to dry out slightly before watering

Cymbidium floribundum. Photo by Manuel Aubron.

MEDIUM Tullock *Cypripedium acaule* mix

pH 5–6

IRRIGATION This plant requires constant moisture during the growing season.

FERTILIZATION Fertilize weekly with half-strength commercial tropical orchid fertilizer from March to October. Do not fertilize from November to February.

MULCH No mulching is necessary.

COMMERCIAL AVAILABILITY The genus includes many commercially important species and hybrids.

COMMENTS Growing at elevations up to 9185 feet and widely cultivated in China and Japan, this cymbidium is a major hybridizing parent in the creation of "miniature" cymbidiums such as C. 'Golden Elf'. It is lithophytic in pine forests and therefore could possibly share garden space beside *Cypripedium acaule*. Also known as *Cymbidium pumilum*, *C. floribundum* produces an albino form valued in horticulture.

REFERENCES Cribb and Bailes 1989, Pridgeon 1992

Cymbidium goeringii

NATIVE HABITAT China and Japan

SEASON OF BLOOM Spring

BLOOM COLOR Green with a white lip marked in purple

HARDINESS Zone 10 (minimum temperature 38°F)

SITING & EXPOSURE Partial sun

DRAINAGE Allow to dry out slightly before watering

MEDIUM Tullock *Cypripedium acaule* mix

pH 5–6

IRRIGATION This plant requires constant moisture during the growing season.

FERTILIZATION Fertilize weekly with half-strength commercial tropical orchid fertilizer from March to October. Do not fertilize from November to February.

MULCH No mulching is necessary.

COMMERCIAL AVAILABILITY The genus includes many commercially important species and hybrids.

COMMENTS Also known as *C. virens*, and available in both albino and variegated forms, this species has been used in horticulture for more than twenty-five hundred years and consequently can be found in

Cymbidium goeringii. Photo by Dick Cavender.

many hybrids and varieties. Found in coniferous forests, it needs an acid medium. It is considered easy to grow and remains manageably small.

REFERENCES Cribb and Bailes 1989, Pridgeon 1992

Cymbidium kanran

NATIVE HABITAT China, Taiwan, Japan, and Korea

SEASON OF BLOOM Variable

BLOOM COLOR Green with purple markings on the lip

HARDINESS Zone 10 (minimum temperature 38°F)

SITING & EXPOSURE Partial sun

DRAINAGE Allow to dry out slightly before watering

MEDIUM Cribb and Bailes (1989) Australian terrestrial mix or Cribb and Bailes (1989) terrestrial mix

pH 5–6

IRRIGATION This plant requires constant moisture during the growing season.

FERTILIZATION Fertilize weekly with half-strength commercial tropical orchid fertilizer from March to October. Do not fertilize from November to February.

MULCH No mulching is necessary.

COMMERCIAL AVAILABILITY The genus includes many commercially important species and hybrids.

COMMENTS Growing at elevations up to 5905 feet in hardwood forests, this species produces a strong fragrance, for which it is valued as a hybridizer.

REFERENCES Cribb and Bailes 1989

Cypripedium acaule

Pink lady's slipper, moccasin flower

NATIVE HABITAT Eastern North America

SEASON OF BLOOM Spring

BLOOM COLOR pink, rarely white

HARDINESS Zones 3–8

SITING & EXPOSURE Dappled shade is the optimum condition for flowering. Although the plants tolerate full sun, they seldom look their best or bloom poorly, even with adequate moisture. (As with most plants, the further north they are grown the more summer sun they can tolerate.) Too much shade results in lush, dark green leaves and few blooms. The tall, top-heavy flower stems should receive protection from prevailing winds.

DRAINAGE Good drainage is essential. On a sloping site the plants can literally be placed atop bare clay soil and covered with the recommended growing mix. On a level site the best approach is to create a raised bed at least 8 inches deep with a 4-inch-deep drainage layer of crushed brick, pumice chunks, or pebbles. Avoid smooth, rounded pebbles and lime-containing materials such as marl or limestone. Fill the bed to the top with growing mix.

MEDIUM Tullock *Cypripedium acaule* mix or Durkee (2000) *C. acaule* mix

pH 4–5

IRRIGATION Natural rainfall is sufficient during most years. Since raised planting beds tend to dry out quickly, irrigation may be needed. Acidify the irrigation water, which should be low in dissolved minerals, with 1 ounce of vinegar per gallon.

FERTILIZATION Do not fertilize.

MULCH Apply a 1-inch layer of partially decomposed pine bark, pine needles, or coarse pine chips, or a combination of these, after the leaves die back.

Cypripedium acaule blooms in May in a shady pine-oak forest in Lewis County, Kentucky.

COMMERCIAL AVAILABILITY See "Suppliers and Organizations."
COMMENTS Traditionally considered a challenge to cultivate, this species thrives with an appropriate medium and strongly acidic conditions. In the wild it often colonizes level sites, where the roots grow in a few inches of compost atop clay.
REFERENCES Cribb 1997, Cribb and Bailes 1989, Durkee 2000

Cypripedium californicum
California lady's slipper
NATIVE HABITAT Northern California and southern Oregon
SEASON OF BLOOM Late spring
BLOOM COLOR White or green
HARDINESS Zones 8–9
SITING & EXPOSURE Partial shade
DRAINAGE Requires bog conditions
MEDIUM Tullock general purpose mix

Cypripedium californicum. Photo by Philip Keenan.

135

pH 5–6

IRRIGATION Plants should not be allowed to completely dry out.

FERTILIZATION Apply commercial orchid fertilizer at half strength every two weeks during the growing season.

MULCH Apply a 1-inch layer of any suitable material, preferably of coniferous origin, after the leaves die back.

COMMERCIAL AVAILABILITY See "Suppliers and Organizations." Seedlings are occasionally available commercially.

COMMENTS This species is easy to cultivate. It grows best planted in the wettest area of the bog garden, short of immersion of the roots, but will adapt to drier conditions. It is often found growing near *Darlingtonia californica*, an insectivorous plant also known as cobra lily or California pitcher plant, on rocky, acidic soils.

REFERENCES Coleman 1995, Cribb and Bailes 1989

Cypripedium formosanum. Photo courtesy of the Global Book Publishing Photo Library.

Cypripedium formosanum

NATIVE HABITAT Southeast Asia

SEASON OF BLOOM Spring

BLOOM COLOR White with pink blush on the lip and a hot pink column

HARDINESS Zones 6–7

SITING & EXPOSURE Partial shade

DRAINAGE Requires bog conditions

MEDIUM Tullock general purpose mix

pH 5–6

IRRIGATION This orchid should be grown in a slightly drier area of the bog bed.

FERTILIZATION Incorporate organic amendments each fall, or feed every other week during the growing season with half-strength commercial orchid fertilizer.

MULCH Apply a 1-inch layer of any suitable material, preferably of coniferous origin, after the leaves die back.

COMMERCIAL AVAILABILITY See "Suppliers and Organizations."

COMMENTS This species is easy to cultivate.

REFERENCES Christian 2003, Fraser and Fraser 2003

Cypripedium japonicum

Japanese lady's slipper

NATIVE HABITAT China and Japan

SEASON OF BLOOM Late spring to early summer

BLOOM COLOR White, pink, or yellow

HARDINESS Zones 8–10

SITING & EXPOSURE Partial sun

DRAINAGE Good drainage is essential. On a sloping site the plants can literally be placed atop bare clay soil and covered with the recommended growing mix. On a level site the best approach is to create a raised bed at least 8 inches deep with a 4-inch-deep drainage layer of crushed brick, pumice chunks, or pebbles. Avoid smooth, rounded pebbles and lime-containing materials such as marl or limestone. Fill the bed to the top with growing mix.

MEDIUM Tullock general purpose mix with added charcoal

pH 5–6

IRRIGATION Natural rainfall is sufficient during most years. Since raised planting beds tend to dry out quickly, irrigation may be needed. Acidify the irrigation water, which should be low in dissolved minerals, with 1 ounce of vinegar per gallon.

FERTILIZATION Incorporate organic amendments each fall, or feed monthly from emergence to frost with half-strength commercial orchid fertilizer.

MULCH Apply a 1-inch layer of any suitable material, preferably of coniferous origin, after the leaves die back.

COMMERCIAL AVAILABILITY See "Suppliers and Organizations."

Cypripedium japonicum. Photo by Manuel Aubron.

COMMENTS Widely cultivated and propagated in Japan, this species makes a good substitute for the more difficult to grow *C. acaule*.

REFERENCES Cribb and Bailes 1989, Fraser and Fraser 2003

Cypripedium kentuckiense
Kentucky lady's slipper

NATIVE HABITAT Mississippi Valley from the coastal plain to Tennessee and Kentucky

Cypripedium kentuckiense. Photo by Jack Carman.

SEASON OF BLOOM Spring

BLOOM COLOR Maroon sepals and petals, pale yellow lip

HARDINESS Zones 6–10

SITING & EXPOSURE Partial shade

DRAINAGE Requires sharp drainage (usually grows along riverbanks and in gullies)

MEDIUM Tullock general purpose mix or pure sand

pH 5–6

IRRIGATION This plant requires constant moisture.

FERTILIZATION Apply commercial orchid fertilizer at half strength every two weeks during the growing season.

MULCH Apply a 1-inch layer of chopped pine needles or oak leaves after the leaves die back.

COMMERCIAL AVAILABILITY See "Suppliers and Organizations."

COMMENTS Although it is listed as an endangered species, *C. kentuckiense* is easily grown and seedlings are available. Plants require four months of cold dormancy.

REFERENCES Whitlow 2003

Cypripedium montanum

Mountain lady's slipper

NATIVE HABITAT From maritime Canada to Alaska and south to Wyoming mountains

SEASON OF BLOOM Late spring

BLOOM COLOR Maroon sepals, white lip with purple veining

HARDINESS Zones 2–5

SITING & EXPOSURE Partial to full shade

DRAINAGE Sharp

MEDIUM Tullock general purpose mix, Tullock general purpose mix with lime, or Cribb and Bailes (1989) bog mix

pH 7–8

IRRIGATION Plants should not be allowed to completely dry out.

FERTILIZATION Apply commercial orchid fertilizer at half strength every two weeks during the growing season.

MULCH Apply a 1-inch layer of any suitable material, preferably of coniferous origin, after the leaves die back.

COMMERCIAL AVAILABILITY See "Suppliers and Organizations."

COMMENTS This orchid is adaptable but may not cope well with hot

Cypripedium montanum. Photo by Philip Keenan.

summers. It is probably best grown in containers in the South. The warmer the weather, the more shade it should receive.

REFERENCES Cribb and Bailes 1989

Cypripedium parviflorum

Small yellow lady's slipper

NATIVE HABITAT From Newfoundland to South Carolina and Georgia

SEASON OF BLOOM Spring

BLOOM COLOR Maroon-striped green sepals and petals, bright yellow lip with red dots

HARDINESS Zones 2–9

SITING & EXPOSURE Partial shade

DRAINAGE Requires bog conditions

MEDIUM Tullock general purpose mix with lime or Cribb and Bailes (1989) bog mix

pH 5–6

IRRIGATION Plants should not be allowed to completely dry out.

FERTILIZATION Apply commercial orchid fertilizer at half strength every two weeks during the growing season.

MULCH Apply a 1-inch layer of any suitable material, preferably of coniferous origin, after the leaves die back.

Cypripedium parviflorum.

COMMERCIAL AVAILABILITY See "Suppliers and Organizations."
COMMENTS *Cypripedium parviflorum* is among the more easily grown
and adaptable species of the genus. It multiplies annually in my garden, and its pleasant roselike fragrance adds to its appeal.
REFERENCES Cribb and Bailes 1989, Whitlow 2003

Cypripedium pubescens

Large yellow lady's slipper
NATIVE HABITAT From Newfoundland to South Carolina and Georgia
SEASON OF BLOOM Spring
BLOOM COLOR Maroon-striped green sepals and petals, bright yellow lip
with red dots
HARDINESS Zones 2–9
SITING & EXPOSURE Partial shade
DRAINAGE Requires bog conditions
MEDIUM Tullock general purpose
mix with lime or Cribb and
Bailes (1989) bog mix
pH 7–8
IRRIGATION Plants should not be
allowed to completely dry out.
FERTILIZATION Apply commercial
orchid fertilizer at half strength
every two weeks during the
growing season.
MULCH Apply a 1-inch layer of
any suitable material, preferably of coniferous origin, after
the leaves die back.
COMMERCIAL AVAILABILITY See
"Suppliers and Organizations."
COMMENTS This is another easily
grown and adaptable *Cypripedium*. It has larger flowers
and a taller growth habit than
C. *parviflorum*, which it otherwise resembles in all respects. A
favorite in my bog garden.

Cypripedium pubescens.

143

REFERENCES Christian 2003, Cribb and Bailes 1989, Fraser and Fraser 2003, Whitlow 2003

Cypripedium reginae

Showy lady's slipper

NATIVE HABITAT From maritime Canada to Tennessee, and in North Carolina mountains

SEASON OF BLOOM Spring

BLOOM COLOR White sepals and petals, white lip with bright pink blush

HARDINESS Zones 2–7

SITING & EXPOSURE Partial shade

DRAINAGE Requires bog conditions

MEDIUM Tullock general purpose mix with lime or Cribb and Bailes (1989) bog mix

pH 6–8

IRRIGATION This species tolerates more water than most cypripediums. Plants should not be allowed to completely dry out.

FERTILIZATION Apply commercial orchid fertilizer at half strength every two weeks during the growing season.

MULCH Apply a 1-inch layer of any suitable material, preferably of coniferous origin, after the leaves die back.

Cypripedium reginae.

COMMERCIAL AVAILABILITY See "Suppliers and Organizations."

COMMENTS Though rare in the warmer South, *C. reginae* is the state flower of Minnesota. It is easily grown in a shady bog at neutral pH. If the pH is too low, it may exhibit tip burn.

REFERENCES Christian 2003, Cribb and Bailes 1989, Fraser and Fraser 2003, Whitlow 2003

Dactylorhiza elata

Marsh orchid

NATIVE HABITAT From southwestern Europe to North Africa

SEASON OF BLOOM Late spring to early summer

BLOOM COLOR Deep purple

HARDINESS Zones 7–10

SITING & EXPOSURE Light shade

DRAINAGE Requires bog conditions

MEDIUM Tullock general purpose mix

pH 5–6

IRRIGATION Plants should not be allowed to completely dry out.

FERTILIZATION Apply commercial orchid fertilizer at half strength every two weeks during the growing season.

MULCH Apply a 1-inch layer of any suitable material, preferably of coniferous origin, after the leaves die back.

COMMERCIAL AVAILABILITY See "Suppliers and Organizations."

COMMENTS Although I have not grown this species, I suspect it would perform for me as *D. fuchsii* has done. The genus does not appear to enjoy summer heat.

REFERENCES Beyrle 2003, Christian 2003, Cribb and Bailes 1989

Dactylorhiza fuchsii

Common spotted orchid

NATIVE HABITAT Great Britain

SEASON OF BLOOM Late spring

BLOOM COLOR Pink

HARDINESS Zones 6–10

SITING & EXPOSURE Light shade to full sun

DRAINAGE Requires bog conditions

MEDIUM Tullock general purpose mix or Tullock general purpose mix with lime

Dactylorhiza fuchsii. Photo by Dick Cavender.

pH 5–6

IRRIGATION Plants should not be allowed to completely dry out.

FERTILIZATION Apply commercial orchid fertilizer at half strength every two weeks during the growing season.

MULCH Apply a 1-inch layer of any suitable material, preferably of coniferous origin, after the leaves die back.

COMMERCIAL AVAILABILITY See "Suppliers and Organizations."

COMMENTS Considered among the easiest of terrestrial orchids, this species is naturalized in some areas of North America. It has grown well in my bog garden.

REFERENCES Beyrle 2003, Christian 2003, Cribb and Bailes 1989, Fraser and Fraser 2003

Dactylorhiza maculata
Heath spotted orchid

NATIVE HABITAT Europe

SEASON OF BLOOM Late spring to early summer

BLOOM COLOR Rose-pink

HARDINESS Zones 3–10

SITING & EXPOSURE Light shade

DRAINAGE Requires bog conditions

MEDIUM Tullock general purpose mix

pH 5–6

IRRIGATION Plants should not be allowed to completely dry out.

FERTILIZATION Apply commercial orchid fertilizer at half strength every two weeks during the growing season.

MULCH Apply a 1-inch layer of any suitable material, preferably of coniferous origin, after the leaves die back.

COMMERCIAL AVAILABILITY See "Suppliers and Organizations."

COMMENTS This species is easy to cultivate. At least one cultivar is available from European growers.

REFERENCES Beyrle 2003, Christian 2003, Cribb and Bailes 1989, Fraser and Fraser 2003

Disa uniflora

NATIVE HABITAT South Africa

SEASON OF BLOOM Winter (summer-dormant)

BLOOM COLOR Red

Disa uniflora. Photo courtesy of the Global Book Publishing Photo Library.

HARDINESS Zone 10 (minimum temperature 38°F)

SITING & EXPOSURE Partial sun or alpine greenhouse

DRAINAGE Requires bog conditions

MEDIUM Pure sand, sand with peat and sphagnum (Pridgeon 1992), or a mixture of long-fiber sphagnum moss and coarse perlite (Cribb and Bailes 1989)—the medium itself makes no difference as long as it never dries out completely

pH 5–6

IRRIGATION Plants should not be allowed to completely dry out.

FERTILIZATION Apply commercial orchid fertilizer at half strength every two weeks during the growing season.

MULCH No mulching is necessary.

COMMERCIAL AVAILABILITY See "Suppliers and Organizations."

COMMENTS This species is considered difficult in cultivation, but many hybrids have been created that offer more promise. Plants require water with a low mineral content.

REFERENCES Beyrle 2003, Cribb and Bailes 1989

Eleorchis japonica

NATIVE HABITAT Japan

SEASON OF BLOOM Spring

BLOOM COLOR Rose-purple or pink

HARDINESS Unknown

SITING & EXPOSURE Partial sun

DRAINAGE Requires bog conditions

MEDIUM 50 percent sand, 50 percent peat moss

pH 5–6

IRRIGATION This plant requires constant moisture.

FERTILIZATION Incorporate organic amendments each fall, or feed monthly from emergence to blooming with half-strength commercial orchid fertilizer.

MULCH Apply a thin layer of grass clippings or chopped pine needles during dormancy.

COMMERCIAL AVAILABILITY See "Suppliers and Organizations."

COMMENTS This species is widely cultivated in Japan.

REFERENCES Cribb and Bailes 1989, Fraser and Fraser 2003, Whitlow 2003

Epipactis gigantea

Western false hellebore

NATIVE HABITAT Europe, but established in the Pacific Northwest

SEASON OF BLOOM Summer

BLOOM COLOR Brown, yellow, and reddish

HARDINESS Zones 3–6

SITING & EXPOSURE Full sun

DRAINAGE Requires bog conditions

MEDIUM Tullock general purpose mix

pH 5–6

IRRIGATION This plant requires constant moisture.

FERTILIZATION Feed lightly with soluble orchid fertilizer during the growing season, or incorporate organic amendments in the growing bed.

MULCH Apply a 1-inch layer of an-suitable material after dormancy.

COMMERCIAL AVAILABILITY See "Suppliers and Organizations."

COMMENTS As with many established exotics, this species is adaptable and worth a try by most hardy orchid fanciers. I found no commercial sources in the United States, but wild plants, which are being introduced, are not protected and should be available from salvage. This orchid is capable of self-seeding in the garden.

REFERENCES Cribb and Bailes 1989, Fraser and Fraser 2003

Epipactis gigantea. Photo by Philip Keenan.

Epipactis helleborine

Eastern false hellebore

NATIVE HABITAT Europe, but established in the eastern United States

SEASON OF BLOOM Summer

BLOOM COLOR Greenish sepals and petals, pale lip marked with pink

HARDINESS Zones 3–7

SITING & EXPOSURE Full sun

DRAINAGE Requires bog conditions

MEDIUM Tullock general purpose mix

pH 5–6

IRRIGATION This plant requires constant moisture.

FERTILIZATION Feed lightly with soluble orchid fertilizer during the growing season, or incorporate organic amendments in the growing bed.

MULCH Apply a 1-inch layer of any suitable material after dormancy.

COMMERCIAL AVAILABILITY See "Suppliers and Organizations."

COMMENTS This species is in all respects similar to *E. gigantea*. It may not do well where summers are hot.

REFERENCES Fraser and Fraser 2003

Galearis spectabilis blooms along Angel Falls Trail, Big South Fork National River and Recreation Area, Scott County, Tennessee.

Galearis spectabilis

Showy orchid

NATIVE HABITAT From the upper Midwest to eastern Canada and the mid South

SEASON OF BLOOM Spring

BLOOM COLOR Magenta with a white lip

HARDINESS Zones 3–8

SITING & EXPOSURE Dappled shade

DRAINAGE Requires sharp drainage, with some moisture retention

MEDIUM Tullock general purpose mix with lime

pH 6–7

IRRIGATION Plants should not be allowed to completely dry out.

FERTILIZATION This species does not like chemical fertilizers. Amend the growing area in fall with organic materials such as blood and bone meal, compost, and chopped leaves.

MULCH Apply a 1-inch layer of any suitable material after the leaves die back.

COMMERCIAL AVAILABILITY See "Suppliers and Organizations."

COMMENTS This species, also known as *Orchis spectabilis*, is more common in the southern part of its range. I've often found it in Tennessee growing in limestone gravel at the edges of roads and parking lots in parks and forests. Among other parts of the South, it's been found growing in a railroad bed in West Virginia.

REFERENCES Bentley 2000, Fraser and Fraser 2003

Goodyera pubescens
Downy rattlesnake plantain

NATIVE HABITAT Eastern United States (except northern Maine) and subtropical South

SEASON OF BLOOM Late summer

BLOOM COLOR White

HARDINESS Zones 2–9

SITING & EXPOSURE Dappled to full shade

DRAINAGE Good drainage is essential. On a sloping site the plants can literally be placed atop bare clay soil and covered with the recommended growing mix. On a level site the best approach is to create a raised bed at least 8 inches deep with a 4-inch-deep drainage layer of crushed brick, pumice chunks, or pebbles. Avoid smooth, rounded pebbles and lime-containing materials such as marl or limestone. Fill the bed to the top with growing mix.

MEDIUM Tullock general purpose mix, Tullock *Cypripedium acaule* mix, Durkee (2000) *C. acaule* mix, or Cribb and Bailes (1989) bog mix

pH 5–6

IRRIGATION Natural rainfall is sufficient during most years. Since raised planting beds tend to dry out quickly, irrigation may be needed. Acidify the irrigation water, which should be low in dissolved minerals, with 1 ounce of vinegar per gallon.

FERTILIZATION This species does not like chemical fertilizers. Top dress the growing area in fall with blood and bone meal.

MULCH Do not cover the evergreen rosette of leaves. Add a thin layer of pine needles or bark chips in fall.

Goodyera pubescens blooms near Ozone Falls, Cumberland County, Tennessee, in July.

A colony of *Goodyera pubescens* along the Maddron Bald Trail, Great Smoky Mountains National Park.

COMMERCIAL AVAILABILITY See "Suppliers and Organizations."

COMMENTS This is perhaps the commonest and most widespread orchid in North America. I prefer to grow it with *C. acaule*, though in more shade.

REFERENCES Christian 2003, Cribb and Bailes 1989, Fraser and Fraser 2003

Goodyera repens

Lesser rattlesnake plantain

NATIVE HABITAT Circumboreal, south in the United States to the Appalachians

SEASON OF BLOOM Late summer

BLOOM COLOR White

HARDINESS Zones 2–7

SITING & EXPOSURE Dappled to full shade

DRAINAGE Good drainage is essential. On a sloping site the plants can literally be placed atop bare clay soil and covered with the recommended growing mix. On a level site the best approach is to create a raised bed at least 8 inches deep with a 4-inch-deep drainage layer of crushed brick, pumice chunks, or pebbles. Avoid smooth, rounded pebbles and lime-containing materials such as marl or limestone. Fill the bed to the top with growing mix.

MEDIUM Tullock general purpose mix, Tullock *Cypripedium acaule* mix, Durkee (2000) *C. acaule* mix, or Cribb and Bailes (1989) bog mix

pH 5–6

IRRIGATION Natural rainfall is sufficient during most years. Since raised planting beds tend to dry out quickly, irrigation may be needed. Acidify the irrigation water, which should be low in dissolved minerals, with 1 ounce of vinegar per gallon.

FERTILIZATION This species does not like chemical fertilizers. Top dress the growing area in fall with blood and bone meal.

MULCH Do not cover the evergreen rosette of leaves. Add a thin layer of pine needles or bark chips in fall.

COMMERCIAL AVAILABILITY This species is not available.

COMMENTS Although this species is common in some habitats, commercial propagation has not been attempted, to my knowledge, and I have never seen wild plants for sale. It might turn up mixed with collected *G. pubescens* from northern locations. It seems to frequent cooler sites and would probably not do well in the South without greenhouse protection.

Gymnadenia conopsea

Fragrant orchid

NATIVE HABITAT Europe and Asia

SEASON OF BLOOM Spring

BLOOM COLOR Pinkish purple

HARDINESS Zones 5–9

SITING & EXPOSURE Full sun to light shade

DRAINAGE Prefers bog conditions

MEDIUM Tullock general purpose mix with lime

pH 7–8

IRRIGATION This plant requires constant moisture.

FERTILIZATION Incorporate organic amendments each fall, or feed every other week during the growing season with half-strength commercial orchid fertilizer.

MULCH Apply a 1-inch layer of any suitable material after the leaves die back.

COMMERCIAL AVAILABILITY See "Suppliers and Organizations."

COMMENTS This species is easy to cultivate and emits a fragrance similar to cloves. Fraser's Thimble Farms offers a hybrid with *Dactylorhiza fuchsii*.

REFERENCES Cribb and Bailes 1989, Fraser and Fraser 2003

Liparis liliifolia

Lily-leaved twayblade

NATIVE HABITAT From the Midwest to the upper South

SEASON OF BLOOM Summer

BLOOM COLOR Greenish sepals, mauve to brownish lip and petals

HARDINESS Zones 3–8

SITING & EXPOSURE Shade

Liparis liliifolia. Photo by Jack Carman.

DRAINAGE Prefers bog conditions but is adaptable

MEDIUM Tullock general purpose mix

pH 5–6

IRRIGATION Plants should not be allowed to dry out during the growing season.

FERTILIZATION Incorporate organic amendments each fall, or feed every other week during the growing season with half-strength commercial orchid fertilizer. Prefers rich sites.

MULCH Apply a 1-inch layer of any suitable material in fall.

COMMERCIAL AVAILABILITY This species is not available.

COMMENTS Bentley (2000) regards this species as more common than generally believed because of its inconspicuousness. I know of no commercial sources, and the plant is not showy enough, probably, to encourage production. A specimen transplanted by a friend proved easy to grow in shade to partial sun in bog conditions. Whitlow (2003) suggests growing it under the same conditions as *Cypripedium kentuckiense*.

REFERENCES Bentley 2000, Whitlow 2003

Ophrys apifera
Bee orchid

NATIVE HABITAT Europe (especially the Mediterranean region), North Africa, and the Near East

SEASON OF BLOOM Winter (summer-dormant)

BLOOM COLOR Greenish to pink with a yellow-spotted chestnut lip

HARDINESS Zones 6–10

SITING & EXPOSURE Full sun to light shade

DRAINAGE Sharp

MEDIUM Tullock general purpose mix with lime

pH 6–7

IRRIGATION Plants should be kept moist during active growth and dry during dormancy.

FERTILIZATION This plant will benefit from light applications during the growing season.

MULCH No mulching is necessary.

COMMERCIAL AVAILABILITY See "Suppliers and Organizations."

COMMENTS Although this orchid grows in full sun to light shade, pot cultivation in an alpine greenhouse is recommended in North America, as it is intolerant of damp cold. Allow tubers to dry in pots during dormancy, and repot in fall. This species shows up in lawns and fields on limestone soils.

REFERENCES Beyrle 2003, Christian 2003, Cribb and Bailes 1989, Fraser and Fraser 2003, Pridgeon 1992

Ophrys fusca

Dull bee orchid

NATIVE HABITAT Europe (especially the Mediterranean region)

SEASON OF BLOOM Winter (summer-dormant)

BLOOM COLOR Green with a brown and yellow lip

HARDINESS Zones 6–10

SITING & EXPOSURE Full sun to light shade

DRAINAGE Sharp

MEDIUM Tullock *Cypripedium acaule* mix

pH 6–7

IRRIGATION Plants should be kept moist during active growth and dry during dormancy.

Ophrys apifera. Photo by Dick Cavender.

FERTILIZATION This plant will benefit from light applications during the growing season.

MULCH No mulching is necessary.

COMMERCIAL AVAILABILITY See "Suppliers and Organizations."

COMMENTS Although this orchid grows in full sun to light shade, pot cultivation in an alpine greenhouse is recommended in North America, as it is intolerant of damp cold. Allow tubers to dry in pots during dormancy, and repot in fall. This species flowers from February to April, depending upon latitude. It is found in dry pine woods and would probably respond well to the conditions favored by *Cypripedium acaule*.

REFERENCES Beyrle 2003, Christian 2003, Cribb and Bailes 1989, Fraser and Fraser 2003, Pridgeon 1992

Ophrys holoserica
Bee orchid

NATIVE HABITAT Europe (especially the Mediterranean region)

SEASON OF BLOOM Winter (summer-dormant)

BLOOM COLOR Highly variable, basically pink with a brown lip

HARDINESS Zones 6–10

SITING & EXPOSURE Full sun to light shade

DRAINAGE Sharp

MEDIUM Tullock general purpose mix with lime

pH 6–7

IRRIGATION Plants should be kept moist during active growth and dry during dormancy.

FERTILIZATION This plant will benefit from light applications during the growing season.

MULCH No mulching is necessary.

COMMERCIAL AVAILABILITY See "Suppliers and Organizations."

COMMENTS Although this orchid grows in full sun to light shade, pot cultivation in an alpine greenhouse is recommended in North America, as it is intolerant of damp cold. Allow tubers to dry in pots during dormancy, and repot in fall.

REFERENCES Beyrle 2003, Christian 2003, Cribb and Bailes 1989, Fraser and Fraser 2003, Pridgeon 1992

Ophrys insectifera
Bee orchid

NATIVE HABITAT Europe (especially the Mediterranean region), North Africa, and the Near East

SEASON OF BLOOM Winter (summer-dormant)

BLOOM COLOR Blue-green with a brown to violet lip

HARDINESS Zones 6–10

SITING & EXPOSURE Full sun to light shade

DRAINAGE Sharp

MEDIUM Tullock general purpose mix with lime

pH 6–7

IRRIGATION Plants should be kept moist during active growth and dry during dormancy.

FERTILIZATION This plant will benefit from light applications during the growing season.

MULCH No mulching is necessary.

COMMERCIAL AVAILABILITY See "Suppliers and Organizations."

COMMENTS Insect mimicry is apparent in this fine example, which occurs farther north than any other member of the genus. Although this orchid grows in full sun to light shade, pot cultivation in an alpine greenhouse is recommended in North America, as it is intolerant of damp cold. Allow tubers to dry in pots during dormancy, and repot in fall.

REFERENCES Beyrle 2003, Christian 2003, Cribb and Bailes 1989, Fraser and Fraser 2003, Pridgeon 1992

Ophrys lutea

Yellow bee orchid

NATIVE HABITAT Europe (especially the Mediterranean region)

SEASON OF BLOOM Winter (summer-dormant)

BLOOM COLOR Green with a bright yellow lip bearing a brown spot

HARDINESS Zones 6–10

SITING & EXPOSURE Full sun to light shade

DRAINAGE Sharp

MEDIUM Tullock general purpose mix with lime

pH 6–7

IRRIGATION Plants should be kept moist during active growth and dry during dormancy.

FERTILIZATION This plant will benefit from light applications during the growing season.

MULCH No mulching is necessary.

COMMERCIAL AVAILABILITY See "Suppliers and Organizations."

COMMENTS Although this orchid grows in full sun to light shade, pot cultivation in an alpine greenhouse is recommended in North America, as it is intolerant of damp cold. Allow tubers to dry in pots during dormancy, and repot in fall.

REFERENCES Beyrle 2003, Christian 2003, Cribb and Bailes 1989, Fraser and Fraser 2003, Pridgeon 1992

Ophrys scolopax

Bee orchid

NATIVE HABITAT Europe (especially the Mediterranean region)

SEASON OF BLOOM Winter (summer-dormant)

BLOOM COLOR Violet-pink and highly variable

HARDINESS Zones 6–10

SITING & EXPOSURE Full sun to light shade

DRAINAGE Sharp

MEDIUM Tullock general purpose mix with lime

pH 6–7

IRRIGATION Plants should be kept moist during active growth and dry during dormancy.

FERTILIZATION This plant will benefit from light applications during the growing season.

MULCH No mulching is necessary.

COMMERCIAL AVAILABILITY See "Suppliers and Organizations."

COMMENTS Although this orchid grows in full sun to light shade, pot cultivation in an alpine greenhouse is recommended in North America, as it is intolerant of damp cold. Allow tubers to dry in pots during dormancy, and repot in fall.

REFERENCES Beyrle 2003, Christian 2003, Cribb and Bailes 1989, Fraser and Fraser 2003, Pridgeon 1992

Ophrys tenthredinifera

Sawfly orchid

NATIVE HABITAT Europe (especially the Mediterranean region), North Africa, and the Near East

SEASON OF BLOOM Winter (summer-dormant)

BLOOM COLOR Pink with a green lip bearing a brown spot

HARDINESS Zones 6–10

SITING & EXPOSURE Full sun to light shade

DRAINAGE Sharp

MEDIUM Tullock general purpose mix with lime

pH 6–7

IRRIGATION Plants should be kept moist during active growth and dry during dormancy.

FERTILIZATION This plant will benefit from light applications during the growing season.

MULCH No mulching is necessary.

COMMERCIAL AVAILABILITY See "Suppliers and Organizations."

COMMENTS Although this orchid grows in full sun to light shade, pot cultivation in an alpine greenhouse is recommended in North America, as it is intolerant of damp cold. Allow tubers to dry in pots during dormancy, and repot in fall. As the common name suggests, this orchid mimics a sawfly.

REFERENCES Beyrle 2003, Christian 2003, Cribb and Bailes 1989, Fraser and Fraser 2003, Pridgeon 1992

Ophrys vernixia

Mirror orchid

NATIVE HABITAT Europe (especially the Mediterranean region)

SEASON OF BLOOM Winter (summer-dormant)

BLOOM COLOR Variable, but usually with striped petals and a shiny blue structure known as the speculum ("mirror" in Latin)

HARDINESS Zones 6–10

SITING & EXPOSURE Full sun to light shade

DRAINAGE Sharp

MEDIUM Tullock general purpose mix with lime

pH 6–7

IRRIGATION Plants should be kept moist during active growth and dry during dormancy.

FERTILIZATION This plant will benefit from light applications during the growing season.

MULCH No mulching is necessary.

COMMERCIAL AVAILABILITY See "Suppliers and Organizations."

COMMENTS Although this orchid grows in full sun to light shade, pot cultivation in an alpine greenhouse is recommended in North America, as it is intolerant of damp cold. Allow tubers to dry in pots during dormancy, and repot in fall. The mimicry of a beetle is unmistakable.

REFERENCES Beyrle 2003, Christian 2003, Cribb and Bailes 1989, Fraser and Fraser 2003, Pridgeon 1992

Orchis mascula

Early purple orchid

NATIVE HABITAT Europe (especially the Mediterranean region)

SEASON OF BLOOM Winter (summer-dormant)

BLOOM COLOR Mauve

HARDINESS Zones 9–10 (minimum temperature 25°F)

SITING & EXPOSURE Full sun to light shade

DRAINAGE Sharp

MEDIUM Tullock general purpose mix

pH 6

IRRIGATION Plants should be kept moist during active growth and dry during dormancy.

FERTILIZATION This plant will benefit from light applications during the growing season.

MULCH No mulching is necessary.

COMMERCIAL AVAILABILITY See "Suppliers and Organizations."

COMMENTS The principal cultural distinction between *Orchis* species and most *Ophrys* species is that *Orchis* is grown in terrestrial compost without added limestone. Be warned: this species produces a scent reminiscent of cat urine.

REFERENCES Beyrle 2003, Christian 2003, Cribb and Bailes 1989, Pridgeon 1992

Orchis militaris

Military orchid

NATIVE HABITAT Europe (especially the Mediterranean region)

SEASON OF BLOOM Winter (summer-dormant)

BLOOM COLOR Mauve

HARDINESS Zones 9–10 (minimum temperature 25°F)

SITING & EXPOSURE Full sun to light shade

DRAINAGE Sharp

MEDIUM Tullock general purpose mix

pH 6

IRRIGATION Plants should be kept moist during active growth and dry during dormancy.

FERTILIZATION This plant will benefit from light applications during the growing season.

MULCH No mulching is necessary.

COMMERCIAL AVAILABILITY See "Suppliers and Organizations."

COMMENTS Formed by the infolding of the sepals and petals, the bloom of this orchid suggests a tiny human.

REFERENCES Beyrle 2003, Christian 2003, Cribb and Bailes 1989, Pridgeon 1992

Orchis morio

Green winged orchid

NATIVE HABITAT Europe (especially the Mediterranean region)

SEASON OF BLOOM Winter (summer-dormant)
BLOOM COLOR Pink, with speckles and splotches of a darker shade
HARDINESS Zones 9–10 (minimum temperature 25°F)
SITING & EXPOSURE Full sun to light shade
DRAINAGE Sharp
MEDIUM Tullock general purpose mix with lime
pH 6
IRRIGATION Plants should be kept moist during active growth and dry during dormancy.
FERTILIZATION This plant will benefit from light applications during the growing season.
MULCH No mulching is necessary.
COMMERCIAL AVAILABILITY See "Suppliers and Organizations."
COMMENTS The sepals and petals are folded to form a "hood" above the striped lip.
REFERENCES Beyrle 2003, Christian 2003, Cribb and Bailes 1989, Pridgeon 1992

Orchis purpurea
Lady orchid

NATIVE HABITAT Europe (especially the Mediterranean region)
SEASON OF BLOOM Winter (summer-dormant)
BLOOM COLOR Reddish purple with a white lip dotted in pink
HARDINESS Zones 9–10 (minimum temperature 25°F)
SITING & EXPOSURE Full sun to light shade
DRAINAGE Sharp
MEDIUM Tullock general purpose mix
pH 6
IRRIGATION Plants should be kept moist during active growth and dry during dormancy.
FERTILIZATION This plant will benefit from light applications during the growing season.
MULCH No mulching is necessary.
COMMERCIAL AVAILABILITY See "Suppliers and Organizations."
COMMENTS The bloom of this orchid resembles a tiny human wearing "harem pants" (Pridgeon 1992).
REFERENCES Beyrle 2003, Christian 2003, Cribb and Bailes 1989, Pridgeon 1992

Orchis simia

Monkey orchid

NATIVE HABITAT Europe (especially the Mediterranean region)

SEASON OF BLOOM Winter (summer-dormant)

BLOOM COLOR White marked and speckled with pink

HARDINESS Zones 9–10 (minimum temperature 25°F)

SITING & EXPOSURE Full sun to light shade

DRAINAGE Sharp

MEDIUM Tullock general purpose mix

pH 6

IRRIGATION Plants should be kept moist during active growth and dry during dormancy.

FERTILIZATION This plant will benefit from light applications during the growing season.

MULCH No mulching is necessary.

COMMERCIAL AVAILABILITY See "Suppliers and Organizations."

COMMENTS The flower, which possesses a three-lobed lip and folded sepals and petals, looks quite like a white monkey with pink hands, feet, and tail.

REFERENCES Beyrle 2003, Christian 2003, Cribb and Bailes 1989, Pridgeon 1992

Platanthera blephariglottis

White fringed orchid

NATIVE HABITAT From the Great Lakes east to Newfoundland, south along the coastal plain to Texas, and in isolated inland locations

SEASON OF BLOOM Late summer

BLOOM COLOR White

HARDINESS Zones 2–10

SITING & EXPOSURE Full sun

DRAINAGE Prefers bog conditions

MEDIUM Tullock general purpose mix or Cribb and Bailes (1989) bog mix

pH 3.5–5

IRRIGATION This plant requires constant moisture.

FERTILIZATION This and other platantheras respond well to biweekly applications of soluble commercial fertilizer from spring emergence until the blooms fade.

Platanthera blephariglottis. Photo by Philip Keenan.

MULCH Apply a 1-inch layer of pine needles, bark chips, or grass clippings after the leaves die back.

COMMERCIAL AVAILABILITY See "Suppliers and Organizations."

COMMENTS *Platanthera blephariglottis* may be likened to a white form of *P. ciliaris*; it is equally adaptable to cultivation in a sunny bog.

REFERENCES Cribb and Bailes 1989, Fraser and Fraser 2003

Platanthera ciliaris

Orange fringed orchid

NATIVE HABITAT From southern Ontario to central Florida

SEASON OF BLOOM Summer

BLOOM COLOR Yellow-orange, orange, or orange-yellow

HARDINESS Zones 4–9

SITING & EXPOSURE At least six hours of sun provides the optimum condition for flowering, and the plants grow fine in full sun. Too much shade results in lush, dark green leaves and few blooms. The tall, top-heavy flower stems should receive protection from prevailing winds, preferably by staking.

A mature *Platanthera ciliaris* produces an impressive flower head.

DRAINAGE Prefers bog conditions

MEDIUM Tullock general purpose mix

pH 4.5–6

IRRIGATION Water level should be maintained at 6–8 inches below the surface of the bog bed.

FERTILIZATION Incorporate organic fertilizers or add timed-release fertilizer to the growing medium annually at the start of the season, or feed monthly with a soluble orchid fertilizer at half the label's recommended dilution. Bog beds fertilized chemically should be thoroughly flushed with fresh water (or by a conveniently timed good rain) prior to each application of fertilizer solution. This step prevents an accumulation of fertilizer salts in the bed, which can damage plants if unchecked.

MULCH Apply a 1-inch layer of partially decomposed pine bark, pine needles, coarse pine chips, or tree leaves, or a combination of these, after the plants die back.

COMMERCIAL AVAILABILITY See "Suppliers and Organizations."

COMMENTS This species is attractive to butterflies and hummingbirds. No two florets on the flower spike are exactly the same. It has proven relatively easy to grow in my garden but forms offsets less readily than other members of the genus.

REFERENCES Cribb and Bailes 1989, Fraser and Fraser 2003

Platanthera cristata

Yellow fringed orchid

NATIVE HABITAT From the southeastern coastal plain to northern Florida

SEASON OF BLOOM Late summer

BLOOM COLOR Orange-yellow

HARDINESS Zones 5–8

SITING & EXPOSURE Full sun

DRAINAGE Prefers bog conditions

MEDIUM Tullock general purpose mix or Cribb and Bailes (1989) bog mix

pH 4–5

IRRIGATION Water level should be maintained at 6–8 inches below the surface of the bog bed.

FERTILIZATION Incorporate organic fertilizers or add timed-release fertilizer to the growing medium annually at the start of the season, or feed

Platanthera cristata. Photo by Philip Keenan.

monthly with a soluble orchid fertilizer at half the label's recommended dilution. Bog beds fertilized chemically should be thoroughly flushed with fresh water (or by a conveniently timed good rain) prior to each application of fertilizer solution. This step prevents an accumulation of fertilizer salts in the bed, which can damage plants if unchecked.

MULCH Apply a 1-inch layer of partially decomposed pine bark, pine needles, coarse pine chips, or tree leaves, or a combination of these, after the plants die back.

COMMERCIAL AVAILABILITY This species is not available.

COMMENTS This species is similar in many respects to *P. ciliaris*, but the inflorescence is more domelike. Given its habitat preferences, it should be as easily grown.

Platanthera flava var. *flava, P. flava* var. *herbiola*

Southern tubercled orchid (var. flava), northern tubercled orchid (var. herbiola)

NATIVE HABITAT From New England to Georgia, depending upon the variety

SEASON OF BLOOM Summer

BLOOM COLOR Yellow-green to maroon-brown, depending upon the variety

HARDINESS Zones 3–8

SITING & EXPOSURE Shade

DRAINAGE Prefers bog conditions

MEDIUM Tullock general purpose mix or Cribb and Bailes (1989) bog mix pH 4.5–5

IRRIGATION Water level should be maintained at 6–8 inches below the surface of the bog bed.

FERTILIZATION Incorporate organic fertilizers or add timed-release fertil-

168

izer to the growing medium annually at the start of the season, or feed monthly with a soluble orchid fertilizer at half the label's recommended dilution. Bog beds fertilized chemically should be thoroughly flushed with fresh water (or by a conveniently timed good rain) prior to each application of fertilizer solution. This step prevents an accumulation of fertilizer salts in the bed, which can damage plants if unchecked.

MULCH Apply a 1-inch layer of partially decomposed pine bark, pine needles, coarse pine chips, or tree leaves, or a combination of these, after the plants die back.

COMMERCIAL AVAILABILITY This species is not available.

COMMENTS This orchid is rather inconspicuous but easily grown and worth it for the pleasing fragrance. In my bog garden, each plant of *P. flava* var. *flava* produces two new plantlets per season.

Platanthera flava var. *flava*, though small, impresses with its floral scent.

Platanthera grandiflora

Large purple fringed orchid

NATIVE HABITAT From southern Ontario east to the Maritimes and south to Tennessee, and in North Carolina mountains

SEASON OF BLOOM Spring

BLOOM COLOR Lavender

HARDINESS Zones 3–8

SITING & EXPOSURE Shade

DRAINAGE Prefers bog conditions

MEDIUM Tullock general purpose mix with lime or Cribb and Bailes (1989) bog mix

pH 7–8

IRRIGATION Water level should be maintained at 6–8 inches below the surface of the bog bed.

169

Platanthera grandiflora blooms along the road to Roan Mountain, Tennessee, in June.

FERTILIZATION Incorporate organic fertilizers or add timed-release fertilizer to the growing medium annually at the start of the season, or feed monthly with a soluble orchid fertilizer at half the label's recommended dilution. Bog beds fertilized chemically should be thoroughly flushed with fresh water (or by a conveniently timed good rain) prior to each application of fertilizer solution. This step prevents an accumulation of fertilizer salts in the bed, which can damage plants if unchecked.

MULCH Apply a 1-inch layer of partially decomposed pine bark, pine needles, coarse pine chips, or tree leaves, or a combination of these, after the plants die back.

COMMERCIAL AVAILABILITY This species is not available.

COMMENTS Not enough is known about this magnificent species. In the Great Smoky Mountains National Park, it grows in habitats similar to those favored by *P. psycodes*, although at higher elevations. This suggests it probably needs cool summer temperatures to do well. Superb in bloom, it produces a strong fragrance similar to lilacs.

REFERENCES Cribb and Bailes 1989

Platanthera integra

Yellow fringeless orchid

NATIVE HABITAT Along the coastal plain from New Jersey to Texas, with isolated populations in Tennessee and North Carolina

SEASON OF BLOOM Summer

BLOOM COLOR Yellow-orange

HARDINESS Zones 5–10

SITING & EXPOSURE Full sun

DRAINAGE Prefers bog conditions

MEDIUM Tullock general purpose mix or Cribb and Bailes (1989) bog mix

Platanthera integra. Photo by Philip Keenan.

pH 4–5

IRRIGATION Water level should be maintained at 6–8 inches below the surface of the bog bed.

FERTILIZATION Incorporate organic fertilizers or add timed-release fertilizer to the growing medium annually at the start of the season, or feed monthly with a soluble orchid fertilizer at half the label's recommended dilution. Bog beds fertilized chemically should be thoroughly flushed with fresh water (or by a conveniently timed good rain) prior to each application of fertilizer solution. This step prevents an accumulation of fertilizer salts in the bed, which can damage plants if unchecked.

MULCH Apply a 1-inch layer of partially decomposed pine bark, pine needles, coarse pine chips, or tree leaves, or a combination of these, after the plants die back.

COMMERCIAL AVAILABILITY This species is not available.

COMMENTS This species often grows alongside other platantheras in the wild, and should do so in the garden.

Platanthera integrilabia

White fringeless orchid, monkey face orchid

NATIVE HABITAT On Cumberland Plateau in Tennessee and in scattered sites in the southwestern Appalachians

SEASON OF BLOOM Summer

BLOOM COLOR White

HARDINESS Zones 7–8

SITING & EXPOSURE Full sun

DRAINAGE Prefers bog conditions

MEDIUM Tullock general purpose mix or Cribb and Bailes (1989) bog mix

pH 4–5

IRRIGATION Water level should be maintained at 6–8 inches below the surface of the bog bed.

FERTILIZATION Incorporate organic fertilizers or add timed-release fertilizer to the growing medium annually at the start of the season, or feed monthly with a soluble orchid fertilizer at half the label's recommended dilution. Bog beds fertilized chemically should be thoroughly flushed with fresh water (or by a conveniently timed good rain) prior to each application of fertilizer solution. This step prevents an accu-

Platanthera integrilabia flourishes in my sunny bog garden.

mulation of fertilizer salts in the bed, which can damage plants if
unchecked.

MULCH Apply a 1-inch layer of partially decomposed pine bark, pine
needles, coarse pine chips, or tree leaves, or a combination of these,
after the plants die back.

COMMERCIAL AVAILABILITY This species is not available.

COMMENTS This orchid is a candidate for federal endangered species
status because of its restricted distribution. Ironically, it is easily cultivated alongside other platantheras in my sunny bog garden. Each
mature plant produces one to three new plantlets each year.

Platanthera peramoena

Purple fringeless orchid

NATIVE HABITAT From Missouri to Pennsylvania, south to Georgia
mountains

SEASON OF BLOOM Late summer

A *Platanthera peramoena* plant that origi-
nated in Missouri blooms in early August.

BLOOM COLOR Hot pink

HARDINESS Zones 5–8

SITING & EXPOSURE Full sun

DRAINAGE Prefers bog conditions

MEDIUM Tullock general purpose mix
or Cribb and Bailes (1989) bog mix

pH 5–6

IRRIGATION Water level should be maintained at 6–8 inches below the surface
of the bog bed.

FERTILIZATION Incorporate organic fertilizers or add timed-release fertilizer
to the growing medium annually at
the start of the season, or feed
monthly with a soluble orchid fertilizer at half the label's recommended
dilution. Bog beds fertilized chemically should be thoroughly flushed
with fresh water (or by a conveniently
timed good rain) prior to each application of fertilizer solution. This step
prevents an accumulation of fertilizer
salts in the bed, which can damage plants if unchecked.

MULCH Apply a 1-inch layer of partially decomposed pine bark, pine
needles, coarse pine chips, or tree leaves, or a combination of these,
after the plants die back.

COMMERCIAL AVAILABILITY This species is not available.

COMMENTS This species is often found growing with *Phlox paniculata* in
open, wet sites. It has proven easy to grow in my bog garden.

REFERENCES Bentley 2000

Platanthera psycodes

Small purple fringed orchid, butterfly orchid

NATIVE HABITAT From the upper Midwest to maritime Canada, south to
Georgia mountains

SEASON OF BLOOM Early spring

BLOOM COLOR Lavender

HARDINESS Zones 3–8

SITING & EXPOSURE Shade

DRAINAGE Prefers bog conditions

MEDIUM Tullock general purpose mix with lime or Cribb and Bailes (1989) bog mix

pH 5–6

IRRIGATION Water level should be maintained at 6–8 inches below the surface of the bog bed.

FERTILIZATION Incorporate organic fertilizers or add timed-release fertilizer to the growing medium annually at the start of the season, or feed monthly with a soluble orchid fertilizer at half the label's recommended dilution. Bog beds fertilized chemically should be thoroughly flushed with fresh water (or by a conveniently timed good rain) prior to each application of fertilizer solution. This step prevents an accumulation of fertilizer salts in the bed, which can damage plants if unchecked.

MULCH Apply a 1-inch layer of partially decomposed pine bark, pine needles, coarse pine chips, or tree leaves, or a combination of these, after the plants die back.

COMMERCIAL AVAILABILITY This species is not available.

COMMENTS This species is not as easily grown in Tennessee as other platantheras, preferring cool conditions. It has adapted reasonably well to a cool, shady spot in my bog garden. It emits a pleasant fragrance similar to cotton candy. See frontispiece for photograph.

REFERENCES Cribb and Bailes 1989

Pleione bulbocodioides

Windowsill orchid

NATIVE HABITAT China

SEASON OF BLOOM Spring

BLOOM COLOR Rose-purple to pink

HARDINESS Zones 7–10 (zone 6 with protection, minimum temperature 15°F)

SITING & EXPOSURE Partial sun

DRAINAGE Allow to dry out slightly before watering, as for a tropical orchid.

MEDIUM Tullock general purpose mix

pH 5–6

IRRIGATION All pleiones need careful watering as roots begin to form in

Pleione bulbocodioides. Photo by Dick Cavender.

spring. Dick Cavender (personal communication) advises, "Warm and wet will rot the sprouts off the bulbs, but cold and wet will not. Warm and moist is just fine."

FERTILIZATION Feed weekly with tropical orchid fertilizer during the growing season only. Flush once a month with plain water to remove accumulated salts.

MULCH Apply 1–3 inches of pine bark chips or pine needles after the first cold snap.

COMMERCIAL AVAILABILITY See "Suppliers and Organizations."

COMMENTS A mountain species usually found with rhododendrons, *P. bulbocodioides* should take well to conditions similar to those recommended for *Cypripedium acaule*. Outdoors it should be placed in a protected spot sheltered from frosts. It is an ideal plant for a cool greenhouse and can be grown in a pot or hanging basket of long-fiber sphagnum moss. Under these conditions, it should be treated like a cool-growing tropical orchid that needs a dry dormant period.

REFERENCES Cavender 2002, Christian 2003, Cribb and Bailes 1989, Fraser and Fraser 2003

176

Pleione Etna (*P. pleionoides* × *P. limprichtii*)

Etna

NATIVE HABITAT Of hybrid origin

SEASON OF BLOOM Spring

BLOOM COLOR Rich rose-purple with red markings on the lip

HARDINESS Unknown

SITING & EXPOSURE Light shade

DRAINAGE Allow to dry out slightly before watering, as for a tropical orchid.

MEDIUM Tullock general purpose mix

pH 5–6

IRRIGATION All pleiones need careful watering as roots begin to form in spring. Dick Cavender (personal communication) advises, "Warm and wet will rot the sprouts off the bulbs, but cold and wet will not. Warm and moist is just fine."

FERTILIZATION Feed weekly with tropical orchid fertilizer during the growing season only. Flush once a month with plain water to remove accumulated salts.

MULCH Apply 1–3 inches of pine bark chips or pine needles after the first cold snap.

COMMERCIAL AVAILABILITY See "Suppliers and Organizations."

COMMENTS Etna is an example of a cross involving *P. limprichtii* that should be tried for winter hardiness in zone 5 south.

REFERENCES Christian 2003, Fraser and Fraser 2003

Pleione formosana

Common windowsill orchid

NATIVE HABITAT Taiwan

SEASON OF BLOOM Spring

BLOOM COLOR Pink, white, and yellow

HARDINESS Zones 7–10

SITING & EXPOSURE Dappled shade

DRAINAGE Allow to dry out slightly before watering, as for a tropical orchid.

MEDIUM Tullock general purpose mix

pH 5–6

IRRIGATION All pleiones need careful watering as roots begin to form in spring. Dick Cavender (personal communication) advises, "Warm and wet will rot the sprouts off the bulbs, but cold and wet will not. Warm and moist is just fine."

FERTILIZATION Feed weekly with tropical orchid fertilizer during the growing season only. Flush once a month with plain water to remove accumulated salts.

MULCH Apply 1–3 inches of pine bark chips or pine needles after the first cold snap.

COMMERCIAL AVAILABILITY See "Suppliers and Organizations."

COMMENTS This orchid is easily grown in a pot in a cool greenhouse, and grows well in a bog garden if the summer weather is not too hot and the moisture level of the growing medium is just right. Warm, wet conditions are to be avoided. A clump of these orchids grew well for several years in a sheltered spot on the north side of my house; they bloomed with the crocuses each spring until an unusually cold winter killed them. Because of its ready availability and ease of culture, this species is an ideal place for half-hardy orchid enthusiasts to begin. It performs well as a houseplant, actually enjoying summer air conditioning if the humidity is maintained, and provides valuable experi-

Pleione formosana flowers reliably in spring in the garden or the cool greenhouse.

ence in dealing with plants having a dormancy requirement. Store *Pleione* bulbs in plastic bags of damp growing mix in the crisper drawer of a refrigerator.

REFERENCES Cavender 2002, Christian 2003, Cribb and Bailes 1989, Fraser and Fraser 2003

Pleione forrestii
Windowsill orchid

NATIVE HABITAT Yunnan (China)

SEASON OF BLOOM Spring

BLOOM COLOR Yellow, often spotted with red

HARDINESS Zones 9–10 (minimum temperature 38°F)

SITING & EXPOSURE Light shade

DRAINAGE Allow to dry out slightly before watering, as for a tropical orchid.

MEDIUM Tullock general purpose mix

pH 5–6

IRRIGATION All pleiones need careful watering as roots begin to form in spring. Dick Cavender (personal communication) advises, "Warm and

Pleione forrestii. Photo by Dick Cavender.

wet will rot the sprouts off the bulbs, but cold and wet will not. Warm and moist is just fine."

FERTILIZATION Feed weekly with tropical orchid fertilizer during the growing season only. Flush once a month with plain water to remove accumulated salts.

MULCH Apply 1–3 inches of pine bark chips or pine needles after the first cold snap.

COMMERCIAL AVAILABILITY See "Suppliers and Organizations."

COMMENTS Considered highly desirable because of its large, yellow flowers, this species is slow to multiply. For this reason, it is usually more costly than similar species.

REFERENCES Cavender 2002, Christian 2003, Cribb and Bailes 1989, Fraser and Fraser 2003

Pleione limprichtii

Windowsill orchid
NATIVE HABITAT Sichuan (China)
SEASON OF BLOOM Spring
BLOOM COLOR Rose-purple with red spots on the lip

Pleione limprichtii. Photo by Manuel Aubron.

HARDINESS Zones 5–10 (minimum temperature –5°F)

SITING & EXPOSURE Light shade

DRAINAGE Allow to dry out slightly before watering, as for a tropical orchid.

MEDIUM Tullock general purpose mix

pH 5–6

IRRIGATION All pleiones need careful watering as roots begin to form in spring. Dick Cavender (personal communication) advises, "Warm and wet will rot the sprouts off the bulbs, but cold and wet will not. Warm and moist is just fine."

FERTILIZATION Feed weekly with tropical orchid fertilizer during the growing season only. Flush once a month with plain water to remove accumulated salts.

MULCH Apply 1–3 inches of pine bark chips or pine needles after the first cold snap.

COMMERCIAL AVAILABILITY See "Suppliers and Organizations."

COMMENTS Many of the more commonly available *Pleione* species have been used to create an array of hybrids. Those with *P. limprichtii* genes should be evaluated for hardiness.

REFERENCES Cavender 2002, Christian 2003, Cribb and Bailes 1989, Fraser and Fraser 2003

Pleione pleionoides

Windowsill orchid

NATIVE HABITAT China

SEASON OF BLOOM Spring

BLOOM COLOR Intense pink with purple and orange markings on the lip

HARDINESS Zones 9–10 (minimum temperature 38°F)

SITING & EXPOSURE Light shade

DRAINAGE Allow to dry out slightly before watering, as for a tropical orchid.

MEDIUM Tullock general purpose mix

pH 5–6

IRRIGATION All pleiones need careful watering as roots begin to form in spring. Dick Cavender (personal communication) advises, "Warm and wet will rot the sprouts off the bulbs, but cold and wet will not. Warm and moist is just fine."

FERTILIZATION Feed weekly with tropical orchid fertilizer during the

Pleione pleionoides. Photo by Manuel Aubron.

The coloration of *Pleione pleionoides* can be quite variable. This plant is a particularly attractive red-lipped form, propagated by Wei-min Lin in Taiwan. Photo by Dick Cavender.

growing season only. Flush once a month with plain water to remove accumulated salts.

MULCH Apply 1–3 inches of pine bark chips or pine needles after the first cold snap.

COMMERCIAL AVAILABILITY See "Suppliers and Organizations."

COMMENTS This species, regarded as easy to grow, often produces two spidery flowers per stem. *Pleione speciosa* is a synonym.

REFERENCES Christian 2003, Fraser and Fraser 2003

Pogonia japonica

Japanese snake mouth orchid

NATIVE HABITAT Japan

SEASON OF BLOOM Late spring

BLOOM COLOR Pink, white, and purple

HARDINESS Zones 9–10 (minimum temperature 32°F)

SITING & EXPOSURE Light shade

DRAINAGE Requires bog conditions

MEDIUM Tullock general purpose mix

pH 5–6

IRRIGATION This plant requires constant moisture.

FERTILIZATION Apply commercial orchid fertilizer at one-quarter
strength monthly from emergence until the flowers fade.

MULCH No mulching is necessary.

COMMERCIAL AVAILABILITY This species may be available from Japan.

COMMENTS This species requires sun, constant moisture, and possibly
winter storage in the refrigerator.

REFERENCES Beyrle 2003, Cribb and Bailes 1989

Pogonia ophioglossoides

Rose pogonia, snake mouth orchid

NATIVE HABITAT From maritime Canada west to Ontario, south through
the Midwest and into Georgia mountains

SEASON OF BLOOM Summer

BLOOM COLOR Hot pink and pale pink with yellow markings

HARDINESS Zones 3–8

SITING & EXPOSURE Full sun

Pogonia ophioglossoides. Photo by Philip Keenan.

DRAINAGE Requires bog conditions
MEDIUM Tullock general purpose mix or Cribb and Bailes (1989) bog mix
pH 4–5
IRRIGATION This plant requires constant moisture.
FERTILIZATION Apply commercial orchid fertilizer at one-quarter
strength monthly from emergence until the flowers fade.
MULCH Apply a thin layer of grass clippings or chopped pine needles.
The plants may also be lifted and stored in damp growing medium in
the refrigerator.
COMMERCIAL AVAILABILITY See "Suppliers and Organizations."
COMMENTS This species requires sun, constant moisture, and possibly
winter storage in the refrigerator. I was able to locate one import
source of propagated plants.
REFERENCES Bentley 2000, Beyrle 2003, Cribb and Bailes 1989, Whit-
low 2003

Ponthieva racemosa. Photo by
Jack Carman.

Ponthieva racemosa

Shadow witch

NATIVE HABITAT Scattered locations from eastern
North America to the Caribbean
SEASON OF BLOOM Fall
BLOOM COLOR Green and white
HARDINESS Zones 5–10
SITING & EXPOSURE Dappled shade
DRAINAGE Requires bog conditions
MEDIUM Tullock general purpose mix with lime
pH 7–8
IRRIGATION Plants should not be allowed to com-
pletely dry out.
FERTILIZATION Feed monthly with half-strength
orchid fertilizer during the growing season.
MULCH Apply a 1-inch layer of any suitable mate-
rial in fall or winter.
COMMERCIAL AVAILABILITY This species is not avail-
able.
COMMENTS Nonresupinate flowers make this plant
unique. It is of interest only to orchid fanciers,

however, as it is not particularly showy and thus has little or no commercial interest.

Pterostylis alobula
Greenhood orchid
NATIVE HABITAT New Zealand
SEASON OF BLOOM Winter (summer-dormant)
BLOOM COLOR Green and white with a red-brown lip
HARDINESS Zones 9–10 (minimum temperature 38°F)
SITING & EXPOSURE Light shade
DRAINAGE Average
MEDIUM Cribb and Bailes (1989) Australian terrestrial mix
pH 5–6
IRRIGATION Plants should be left to almost dry out before receiving water.
FERTILIZATION Feed monthly with quarter-strength commercial orchid fertilizer.
MULCH No mulching is necessary.
COMMERCIAL AVAILABILITY See "Suppliers and Organizations."
COMMENTS Among the most popular of the genus, this orchid is easy to grow and has been propagated in large numbers. It requires acidic conditions.
REFERENCES Beyrle 2003, Cribb and Bailes 1989, Pridgeon 1992

Pterostylis banksii
Greenhood orchid
NATIVE HABITAT New Zealand
SEASON OF BLOOM Winter (summer-dormant)
BLOOM COLOR Green with brown tails on the sepals
HARDINESS Zones 9–10 (minimum temperature 38°F)
SITING & EXPOSURE Light shade
DRAINAGE Average
MEDIUM Cribb and Bailes (1989) Australian terrestrial mix
pH 5–6
IRRIGATION Plants should be left to almost dry out before receiving water.
FERTILIZATION Feed monthly with quarter-strength commercial orchid fertilizer.

MULCH No mulching is necessary.

COMMERCIAL AVAILABILITY See "Suppliers and Organizations."

COMMENTS Among the most popular of the New Zealand species, this orchid is easy to grow and has been propagated in large numbers. It requires acidic conditions and needs more water than the Australian members of the genus.

REFERENCES Beyrle 2003, Cribb and Bailes 1989, Pridgeon 1992

Pterostylis baptistii

Greenhood orchid

NATIVE HABITAT Eastern Australia

SEASON OF BLOOM Winter (summer-dormant)

BLOOM COLOR Green and white with brown markings

HARDINESS Zones 9–10 (minimum temperature 38°F)

SITING & EXPOSURE Light shade

DRAINAGE Average

MEDIUM Cribb and Bailes (1989) Australian terrestrial mix

pH 5–6

IRRIGATION Plants should be left to almost dry out before receiving water.

FERTILIZATION Feed monthly with quarter-strength commercial orchid fertilizer.

MULCH No mulching is necessary.

COMMERCIAL AVAILABILITY See "Suppliers and Organizations."

COMMENTS This species produces the largest flowers of the genus and is considered vigorous and easily cultivated.

REFERENCES Beyrle 2003, Cribb and Bailes 1989, Pridgeon 1992

Pterostylis boormanii

Sikh's whiskers

NATIVE HABITAT Southeastern Australia

SEASON OF BLOOM Winter (summer-dormant)

BLOOM COLOR Dark red

HARDINESS Zones 9–10 (minimum temperature 38°F)

SITING & EXPOSURE Light shade

DRAINAGE Average

MEDIUM Cribb and Bailes (1989) Australian terrestrial mix

pH 5–6

IRRIGATION Plants should be left to almost dry out before receiving water.

FERTILIZATION Feed monthly with quarter-strength commercial orchid fertilizer.

MULCH No mulching is necessary.

COMMERCIAL AVAILABILITY See "Suppliers and Organizations."

COMMENTS This species is found in dry habitats and is not widely cultivated like others of its genus.

REFERENCES Beyrle 2003, Cribb and Bailes 1989, Pridgeon 1992

Pterostylis concinna
Greenhood orchid

NATIVE HABITAT Eastern Australia

SEASON OF BLOOM Winter (summer-dormant)

BLOOM COLOR Green and white with a brown lip

HARDINESS Zones 9–10 (minimum temperature 38°F)

SITING & EXPOSURE Light shade

DRAINAGE Average

MEDIUM Cribb and Bailes (1989) Australian terrestrial mix

pH 5–6

IRRIGATION Plants should be left to almost dry out before receiving water.

FERTILIZATION Feed monthly with quarter-strength commercial orchid fertilizer.

MULCH No mulching is necessary.

COMMERCIAL AVAILABILITY See "Suppliers and Organizations."

COMMENTS Among the most popular of the Australian species, this greenhood is easy to grow and has been propagated in large numbers. As with other species of *Pterostylis*, it requires acidic conditions. A form with yellow-orange flowers is popular with Australian horticulturists.

REFERENCES Beyrle 2003, Cribb and Bailes 1989, Pridgeon 1992

Pterostylis cucullata
Greenhood orchid

NATIVE HABITAT Southern Australia

SEASON OF BLOOM Winter (summer-dormant)

BLOOM COLOR Dark reddish brown with red-brown lip

HARDINESS Zones 9–10 (minimum temperature 38°F)

SITING & EXPOSURE Light shade

DRAINAGE Average

MEDIUM Cribb and Bailes (1989) Australian terrestrial mix
pH 5–6
IRRIGATION Plants should be left to almost dry out before receiving water.
FERTILIZATION Feed monthly with quarter-strength commercial orchid
    fertilizer.
MULCH No mulching is necessary.
COMMERCIAL AVAILABILITY See "Suppliers and Organizations."
COMMENTS Yet another Australian species considered easy to grow. The
    dormancy period is longer than for other members of the genus, a fact
    that must be taken into account in cultivation.
REFERENCES Beyrle 2003, Cribb and Bailes 1989, Pridgeon 1992

Pterostylis curta

Greenhood orchid
NATIVE HABITAT Eastern Australia
SEASON OF BLOOM Winter (summer-dormant)
BLOOM COLOR Green and white with red-brown lip
HARDINESS Zones 9–10 (minimum temperature 38°F)
SITING & EXPOSURE Light shade
DRAINAGE Average
MEDIUM Cribb and Bailes (1989) Australian terrestrial mix
pH 5–6
IRRIGATION Plants should be left to almost dry out before receiving water.
FERTILIZATION Feed monthly with quarter-strength commercial orchid
    fertilizer.
MULCH No mulching is necessary.
COMMERCIAL AVAILABILITY See "Suppliers and Organizations."
COMMENTS This species is large, robust, and easily grown.
REFERENCES Beyrle 2003, Cribb and Bailes 1989, Pridgeon 1992

Pterostylis grandiflora

Greenhood orchid
NATIVE HABITAT Australia
SEASON OF BLOOM Winter (summer-dormant)
BLOOM COLOR Green and white with red-brown lip
HARDINESS Zones 9–10 (minimum temperature 38°F)
SITING & EXPOSURE Light shade
DRAINAGE Average

Pterostylis curta. Photo courtesy of the Global Book Publishing Photo Library.

MEDIUM Cribb and Bailes (1989) Australian terrestrial mix
pH 5–6
IRRIGATION Plants should be left to almost dry out before receiving water.
FERTILIZATION Feed monthly with quarter-strength commercial orchid
fertilizer.
MULCH No mulching is necessary.
COMMERCIAL AVAILABILITY See "Suppliers and Organizations."
COMMENTS This is another *Pterostylis* species that is popular with Australian orchidists.
REFERENCES Beyrle 2003, Cribb and Bailes 1989, Pridgeon 1992

Pterostylis longifolia

Greenhood orchid
NATIVE HABITAT Australia
SEASON OF BLOOM Winter (summer-dormant)
BLOOM COLOR Green
HARDINESS Zones 9–10 (minimum temperature 38°F)
SITING & EXPOSURE Light shade
DRAINAGE Average
MEDIUM Cribb and Bailes (1989) Australian terrestrial mix
pH 5–6
IRRIGATION Plants should be left to almost dry out before receiving water.
FERTILIZATION Feed monthly with quarter-strength commercial orchid
fertilizer.
MULCH No mulching is necessary.
COMMERCIAL AVAILABILITY See "Suppliers and Organizations."
COMMENTS This greenhood is easy to grow but slow to multiply.
REFERENCES Beyrle 2003, Cribb and Bailes 1989, Pridgeon 1992

Pterostylis plumosa

Greenhood orchid
NATIVE HABITAT Australia
SEASON OF BLOOM Winter (summer-dormant)
BLOOM COLOR Green with a yellowish lip
HARDINESS Zones 9–10 (minimum temperature 38°F)
SITING & EXPOSURE Light shade
DRAINAGE Average
MEDIUM Cribb and Bailes (1989) Australian terrestrial mix

pH 5–6

IRRIGATION Plants should be left to almost dry out before receiving water.

FERTILIZATION Feed monthly with quarter-strength commercial orchid fertilizer.

MULCH No mulching is necessary.

COMMERCIAL AVAILABILITY See "Suppliers and Organizations."

COMMENTS This orchid is considered difficult to grow. Its feathery lip is reminiscent of grasses in bloom.

REFERENCES Beyrle 2003, Cribb and Bailes 1989, Pridgeon 1992

Pterostylis rufa
Greenhood orchid

NATIVE HABITAT New South Wales

SEASON OF BLOOM Winter (summer-dormant)

BLOOM COLOR Reddish

HARDINESS Zones 9–10 (minimum temperature 38°F)

SITING & EXPOSURE Light shade

DRAINAGE Average

MEDIUM Cribb and Bailes (1989) Australian terrestrial mix

pH 5–6

IRRIGATION Plants should be left to almost dry out before receiving water.

FERTILIZATION Feed monthly with quarter-strength commercial orchid fertilizer.

MULCH No mulching is necessary.

COMMERCIAL AVAILABILITY See "Suppliers and Organizations."

COMMENTS The flower color suggested the specific epithet, which means "reddish brown." Found in dry forests, this greenhood must be kept completely dry during dormancy.

REFERENCES Beyrle 2003, Cribb and Bailes 1989, Pridgeon 1992

Serapias lingua
Tongue orchid

NATIVE HABITAT Mediterranean Europe and North Africa

SEASON OF BLOOM Winter (summer-dormant)

BLOOM COLOR Greenish to reddish purple with a purple and yellow lip

HARDINESS Zones 8–10 (zone 7 with protection, minimum temperature 15°F)

SITING & EXPOSURE Light shade

DRAINAGE Average

MEDIUM Tullock general purpose mix with added sand, no sphagnum

pH 6

IRRIGATION Plants should be left to almost dry out before receiving water.

FERTILIZATION Feed monthly with quarter-strength commercial orchid fertilizer during the growing season.

MULCH No mulching is necessary.

COMMERCIAL AVAILABILITY See "Suppliers and Organizations."

COMMENTS Easily grown and similar to *Ophrys*, this species should be tried by more North American gardeners. It multiplies quickly to form large clumps. Studies reveal nine other species of similar appearance and culture across the range of the genus.

REFERENCES Beyrle 2003, Cribb and Bailes 1989

Spiranthes cernua var. *odorata* 'Chadd's Ford'

Fragrant nodding lady's tresses

NATIVE HABITAT Throughout eastern North America

SEASON OF BLOOM Late summer to frost

BLOOM COLOR White

HARDINESS Zones 5–10

SITING & EXPOSURE At least six hours of sun provides the optimum condition for flowering, and the plants grow fine in full sun. Too much shade results in lush, dark green leaves and few blooms. The tall, top-heavy flower stems should receive protection from prevailing winds, preferably by staking.

DRAINAGE Will adapt to a moist, well-drained garden soil that supports perennials such as *Lilium*, or can thrive at the edge of a pond with its roots submerged. Grows best in bog conditions.

MEDIUM Tullock general purpose mix

pH 4–5

IRRIGATION Water level should be maintained at 6–8 inches below the surface of the bog bed. In the perennial bed, plants should receive 1 inch of water per week during the growing season, and will accept much more.

FERTILIZATION Incorporate organic fertilizers or add timed-release fertilizer to the growing medium annually at the start of the season, or feed monthly with a soluble orchid fertilizer at half the label's recommended dilution. Bog beds fertilized chemically should be thoroughly flushed with fresh water (or by a conveniently timed good rain) prior to each application of fertilizer solution. This step prevents an accumulation of fertilizer salts in the bed, which can damage plants if unchecked.

MULCH Apply a 1-inch layer of partially decomposed pine bark, pine needles, or coarse pine chips, or a combination of these, after the leaves die back. Dry grass clippings may also be used sparingly as a mulch in the bog garden; they slowly decay over winter and add nitrogen to the medium. The persistent rosette of green leaves should remain uncovered throughout the winter.

COMMERCIAL AVAILABILITY See "Suppliers and Organizations."

COMMENTS This is among the most adaptable and vigorous species in my garden. Each plant annually produces four or five offspring, thus forming a nice clump in a few seasons. A vanilla fragrance adds to the appeal. This makes a good cut flower. See page 102 for photograph.

REFERENCES Cribb and Bailes 1989, Fraser and Fraser 2003, Glick 1995

Spiranthes lacera

Slender lady's tresses

NATIVE HABITAT From the Great Plains to New England, south to Georgia and South Carolina

SEASON OF BLOOM Fall

BLOOM COLOR White

HARDINESS Zones 3–8

SITING & EXPOSURE Full sun to partial shade

DRAINAGE Average

MEDIUM Tullock general purpose mix or Cribb and Bailes (1989) bog mix

pH 5–6

IRRIGATION Plants grow well with about an inch of water per week from spring through fall.

FERTILIZATION This species adapts to relatively poor soils but also responds to weak applications of soluble or organic fertilizers.

MULCH Apply a thin layer of grass clippings to protect the roots and retain moisture.

COMMERCIAL AVAILABILITY This species is not available.

COMMENTS Found in rather dry sites, this species became part of my

Spiranthes lacera. Photo by Philip Keenan.

collection when it turned up in my mother's front lawn. The leaves die back before flowering. It is of interest primarily to orchidists.

REFERENCES Cribb and Bailes 1989

Spiranthes lucida
Shining lady's tresses

NATIVE HABITAT From New England to the upper Midwest, rarely south into the Appalachians

SEASON OF BLOOM Fall

BLOOM COLOR White

HARDINESS Zones 3–8

SITING & EXPOSURE Partial sun

DRAINAGE Prefers bog conditions

MEDIUM Tullock general purpose mix with lime

pH 7–8

IRRIGATION Water level should be maintained at 6–8 inches below the surface of the bog bed. In the perennial bed, plants should receive 1 inch of water per week during the growing season, and will accept much more.

FERTILIZATION Incorporate organic fertilizers or add timed-release fertilizer to the growing medium annually at the start of the season, or feed monthly with a soluble orchid fertilizer at half the label's recommended dilution. Bog beds fertilized chemically should be thoroughly flushed with fresh water (or by a conveniently timed good rain) prior to each application of fertilizer solution. This step prevents an accumulation of fertilizer salts in the bed, which can damage plants if unchecked.

MULCH Apply a 1-inch layer of partially decomposed pine bark, pine needles, or coarse pine chips, or a combination of these, after the leaves die back. Dry grass clippings may also be used sparingly as a mulch in the bog garden; they slowly decay over winter and add nitrogen to

Spiranthes lucida. Photo by Philip Keenan.

the medium. The persistent rosette of green leaves should remain uncovered throughout the winter.

COMMERCIAL AVAILABILITY This species is not available.

COMMENTS This *Spiranthes* species likely has little commercial value. It is found in limestone seeps and similar neutral to alkaline, wet habitats.

Spiranthes ochroleuca

Yellow lady's tresses

NATIVE HABITAT From the eastern United States south to Tennessee and North Carolina

SEASON OF BLOOM Fall

BLOOM COLOR Yellowish cream

HARDINESS Zones 3–7

SITING & EXPOSURE Full sun to partial shade

DRAINAGE Average

MEDIUM Tullock general purpose mix or Cribb and Bailes (1989) bog mix

pH 5–6

IRRIGATION Water level should be maintained at 6–8 inches below the surface of the bog bed. In the perennial bed, plants should receive 1 inch of water per week during the growing season, and will accept much more.

FERTILIZATION Incorporate organic fertilizers or add timed-release fertilizer to the growing medium annually at the start of the season, or feed monthly with a soluble orchid fertilizer at half the label's recommended dilution. Bog beds fertilized chemically should be thoroughly flushed with fresh water (or by a conveniently timed good rain) prior to each application of fertilizer solution. This step prevents an accumulation of fertilizer salts in the bed, which can damage plants if unchecked.

MULCH Apply a 1-inch layer of partially decomposed pine bark, pine needles, or coarse

Spiranthes ochroleuca. Photo by Jack Carman.

196

pine chips, or a combination of these, after the leaves die back. Dry grass clippings may also be used sparingly as a mulch in the bog garden; they slowly decay over winter and add nitrogen to the medium. The persistent rosette of green leaves should remain uncovered throughout the winter.

COMMERCIAL AVAILABILITY This species is not available.

COMMENTS Large and showy, and growing in slightly drier conditions than *S. cernua*, this species should be an excellent garden subject.

REFERENCES Cribb and Bailes 1989

Spiranthes sinensis

Chinese lady's tresses

NATIVE HABITAT Tropical Asia

SEASON OF BLOOM Fall

BLOOM COLOR White

HARDINESS Zones 9–10

SITING & EXPOSURE Full sun to partial shade

DRAINAGE Requires good drainage and plenty of moisture

MEDIUM Tullock general purpose mix or Cribb and Bailes (1989) bog mix

pH 7–8

IRRIGATION Water level should be maintained at 6–8 inches below the surface of the bog bed. In the perennial bed, plants should receive 1 inch of water per week during the growing season, and will accept much more.

FERTILIZATION Incorporate organic fertilizers or add timed-release fertilizer to the growing medium annually at the start of the season, or feed monthly with a soluble orchid fertilizer at half the label's recommended dilution. Bog beds fertilized chemically should be thoroughly flushed with fresh water (or by a conveniently timed good rain) prior to each application of fertilizer solution. This step prevents an accumulation of fertilizer salts in the bed, which can damage plants if unchecked.

MULCH Apply a 1-inch layer of partially decomposed pine bark, pine needles, or coarse pine chips, or a combination of these, after the leaves die back. Dry grass clippings may also be used sparingly as a mulch in the bog garden; they slowly decay over winter and add nitrogen to the medium. The persistent rosette of green leaves should remain uncovered throughout the winter.

COMMERCIAL AVAILABILITY This species is not available, at least within the United States.

COMMENTS Widely cultivated within its native range and easily grown from seed, this species requires an alpine greenhouse for successful culture.

REFERENCES Pridgeon 1992

Spiranthes spiralis

European autumn lady's tresses

NATIVE HABITAT Europe

SEASON OF BLOOM Fall

BLOOM COLOR White

HARDINESS Zones 3–10

SITING & EXPOSURE Full sun

DRAINAGE Requires good drainage, especially in heavier soils

MEDIUM Tullock general purpose mix or Cribb and Bailes (1989) bog mix

pH 7–8

IRRIGATION Water level should be maintained at 6–8 inches below the surface of the bog bed. In the perennial bed, plants should receive 1 inch of water per week during the growing season, and will accept much more.

FERTILIZATION Incorporate organic fertilizers or add timed-release fertilizer to the growing medium annually at the start of the season, or feed monthly with a soluble orchid fertilizer at half the label's recommended dilution. Bog beds fertilized chemically should be thoroughly flushed with fresh water (or by a conveniently timed good rain) prior to each application of fertilizer solution. This step prevents an accumulation of fertilizer salts in the bed, which can damage plants if unchecked.

MULCH Apply a 1-inch layer of partially decomposed pine bark, pine needles, or coarse pine chips, or a combination of these, after the leaves die back. Dry grass clippings may also be used sparingly as a mulch in the bog garden; they slowly decay over winter and add nitrogen to the medium. The persistent rosette of green leaves should remain uncovered throughout the winter.

COMMERCIAL AVAILABILITY This species is not available.

COMMENTS Often cultivated in its home range, this species has eluded my attempts to locate a commercial source. It can be established in turf grass plantings on calcareous soils.

REFERENCES Pridgeon 1992

Spiranthes tuberosa

Little lady's tresses

NATIVE HABITAT The southeastern coastal plain, except southern Florida

SEASON OF BLOOM Late summer

BLOOM COLOR White

HARDINESS Zones 6–9

SITING & EXPOSURE Full sun to partial shade

DRAINAGE Good drainage is essential. On a sloping site the plants can literally be placed atop bare clay soil and covered with the recommended growing mix. On a level site the best approach is to create a raised bed at least 8 inches deep with a 4-inch-deep drainage layer of crushed brick, pumice chunks, or pebbles. Avoid smooth, rounded pebbles and lime-containing materials such as marl or limestone. Fill the bed to the top with growing mix.

MEDIUM Tullock general purpose mix or Cribb and Bailes (1989) bog mix

pH 5–6

Spiranthes tuberosa. Photo by Philip Keenan.

IRRIGATION Natural rainfall is sufficient during most years. Since raised planting beds tend to dry out quickly, irrigation may be needed. Acidify the irrigation water, which should be low in dissolved minerals, with 1 ounce of vinegar per gallon.

FERTILIZATION Do not fertilize.

MULCH Apply a 1-inch layer of partially decomposed pine bark, pine needles, coarse pine chips, or a combination, after the leaves die back.

COMMERCIAL AVAILABILITY This species is not available.

COMMENTS This is another *Spiranthes* that prefers dry sites, but it also grows in rather acidic soils and could be considered as a companion for *Cypripedium acaule*.

Spiranthes vernalis

Spring lady's tresses

NATIVE HABITAT From the Great Plains south to the Gulf and along the coastal plain to Massachusetts

Spiranthes vernalis. Photo by Philip Keenan.

SEASON OF BLOOM Spring to summer, depending upon winter temperatures
BLOOM COLOR White
HARDINESS Zones 3–10
SITING & EXPOSURE Full sun to partial shade
DRAINAGE Prefers bog conditions
MEDIUM Tullock general purpose mix or Cribb and Bailes (1989) bog mix
pH 5–6
IRRIGATION Water level should be maintained at 6–8 inches below the surface of the bog bed. In the perennial bed, plants should receive 1 inch of water per week during the growing season, and will accept much more.
FERTILIZATION Incorporate organic fertilizers or add timed-release fertilizer to the growing medium annually at the start of the season, or feed monthly with a soluble orchid fertilizer at half the label's recommended dilution. Bog beds fertilized chemically should be thoroughly flushed with fresh water (or by a conveniently timed good rain) prior to each application of fertilizer solution. This step prevents an accumulation of fertilizer salts in the bed, which can damage plants if unchecked.
MULCH Apply a 1-inch layer of partially decomposed pine bark, pine needles, or coarse pine chips, or a combination of these, after the leaves die back. Dry grass clippings may also be used sparingly as a mulch in the bog garden; they slowly decay over winter and add nitrogen to the medium. The persistent rosette of green leaves should remain uncovered throughout the winter.
COMMERCIAL AVAILABILITY This species is not available.
COMMENTS The florets of this species, unlike those of most *Spiranthes*, are arranged linearly on the raceme. This is potentially a commercially valuable species because of its bloom time.

Thelymitra carnea
Pink sun orchid
NATIVE HABITAT Eastern Australia
SEASON OF BLOOM Spring to early summer
BLOOM COLOR Rose-pink
HARDINESS Zones 8–10 (minimum temperature 26°F)
SITING & EXPOSURE Light shade to full sun
DRAINAGE Average

MEDIUM Cribb and Bailes (1989) Australian terrestrial mix

pH 5–6

IRRIGATION Plants should be kept moist during active growth and dry during dormancy.

FERTILIZATION Feed lightly and regularly during active growth.

MULCH No mulching is necessary.

COMMERCIAL AVAILABILITY See "Suppliers and Organizations."

COMMENTS While *Thelymitra* species are tricky in cultivation, several beautiful hybrids have proven far easier to grow. Like most summer-dormant species, they will need a cool greenhouse in much of North America. Interestingly, seed is easily germinated on the same growing mix used for the parents.

REFERENCES Beyrle 2003, Cribb and Bailes 1989, Pridgeon 1992

Thelymitra crinita

Sun orchid

NATIVE HABITAT Western Australia

SEASON OF BLOOM Spring to early summer

BLOOM COLOR Blue

HARDINESS Zones 8–10 (minimum temperature 26°F)

SITING & EXPOSURE Light shade to full sun

DRAINAGE Average

MEDIUM Cribb and Bailes (1989) Australian terrestrial mix

pH 5–6

IRRIGATION Plants should be kept moist during active growth and dry during dormancy.

FERTILIZATION Feed lightly and regularly during active growth.

MULCH No mulching is necessary.

COMMERCIAL AVAILABILITY See "Suppliers and Organizations."

COMMENTS While *Thelymitra* species are tricky in cultivation, several beautiful hybrids have proven far easier to grow. Like most summer-dormant species, they will need a cool greenhouse in much of North America.

REFERENCES Beyrle 2003, Cribb and Bailes 1989, Pridgeon 1992

Thelymitra ixiodes

Sun orchid

NATIVE HABITAT Australia

Thelymitra ixiodes. Photo courtesy of the Global Book Publishing Photo Library.

SEASON OF BLOOM Spring

BLOOM COLOR Blue, sometimes tinged with pink

HARDINESS Zones 9–10 (minimum temperature 38°F)

SITING & EXPOSURE Full sun

DRAINAGE Sharp

MEDIUM Cribb and Bailes (1989) Australian terrestrial mix

pH 5–6

IRRIGATION Plants should be kept moist during active growth and dry during dormancy.

FERTILIZATION Feed lightly and regularly during active growth.

MULCH No mulching is necessary.

COMMERCIAL AVAILABILITY See "Suppliers and Organizations."

COMMENTS Like all *Thelymitra* species, this one lacks the highly modified labellum that is characteristic of most orchids, and the flowers thus resemble those of more familiar plants, such as lilies. It needs a cool greenhouse in much of North America.

REFERENCES Beyrle 2003, Cribb and Bailes 1989, Pridgeon 1992

Thelymitra nuda

Sun orchid

NATIVE HABITAT Eastern Australia

SEASON OF BLOOM Spring to early summer

BLOOM COLOR Blue

HARDINESS Zones 8–10 (minimum temperature 26°F)

SITING & EXPOSURE Light shade to full sun

DRAINAGE Average

MEDIUM Cribb and Bailes (1989) Australian terrestrial mix

pH 5–6

IRRIGATION Plants should be kept moist during active growth and dry during dormancy.

FERTILIZATION Feed lightly and regularly during active growth.

MULCH No mulching is necessary.

COMMERCIAL AVAILABILITY See "Suppliers and Organizations."

COMMENTS This species is considered the easiest member of the genus and is widely cultivated in its home range. The flowers are pleasantly scented, another inducement to try it in a frost-free greenhouse.

REFERENCES Beyrle 2003, Cribb and Bailes 1989, Pridgeon 1992

Tipularia discolor
Cranefly orchid

NATIVE HABITAT From the middle of Ohio south along the coastal plain to lower New York and the Florida panhandle

SEASON OF BLOOM Summer

BLOOM COLOR Translucent and monochromic in pale cream, brown, green, or purplish

HARDINESS Zones 5–8

SITING & EXPOSURE Summer shade, winter sun. More specifically, choose a site with dappled shade in winter and full shade in summer. The plants should receive protection from prevailing winds.

DRAINAGE Good drainage is essential.

MEDIUM Tullock *Cypripedium acaule* mix, Durkee (2000) *C. acaule* mix, or Tullock general purpose mix

pH 5–6

Tipularia discolor. Photo by Jack Carman.

IRRIGATION Natural rainfall is sufficient during most years. Since raised planting beds tend to dry out quickly, irrigation may be needed. Acidify the irrigation water, which should be low in dissolved minerals, with 1 ounce of vinegar per gallon.

FERTILIZATION Do not fertilize.

MULCH Apply a 1-inch layer of partially decomposed pine bark, pine needles, or coarse pine chips, or a combination of these, after the winter leaf emerges. Take care not to smother the winter leaf.

COMMERCIAL AVAILABILITY See "Suppliers and Organizations."

COMMENTS While its flower is not showy, this plant has strong winter interest due to its unusual overwintering leaf, which bears an interesting texture and deep purple coloration. The winter leaf dies down before blooming, usually in July; it disappears by early summer, and the flower spike appears in August, resembling a cluster of craneflies hovering. This species is adaptable as long as the soil is well drained and there is winter moisture.

REFERENCES Cribb and Bailes 1989, Glick 1995

Triphora trianthophora

Three birds orchid

NATIVE HABITAT From New England to the Gulf Coast

SEASON OF BLOOM Summer

BLOOM COLOR Pink, white, and green

HARDINESS Zones 4–9

SITING & EXPOSURE Shade

DRAINAGE Requires bog conditions

MEDIUM Tullock general purpose mix or Cribb and Bailes (1989) bog mix

pH 5.5–7

IRRIGATION This plant requires constant moisture.

FERTILIZATION Requirements are not known.

MULCH Apply chopped pine or hemlock needles to mimic the conditions
of natural sites.

COMMERCIAL AVAILABILITY This species is not available.

COMMENTS This attractive, unusual orchid is easily cultivated and
coaxed into bloom. Although exactly what triggers blooming is
poorly understood, a drop of approximately ten degrees will result in
flowering two days later. Often, all plants in an area exposed to similar meteorological conditions will flower in concert.

REFERENCES Bentley 2000

Triphora trianthophora. Photo by Philip Keenan.

Epilogue

I ALLUDED IN CHAPTER 1 TO THE FACT THAT MY TRAINING and experience as an ichthyologist and aquatic biologist have informed most of my thinking about orchid conservation. Several anecdotes from my past should serve to illustrate the practicalities of biodiversity preservation in the watery realm, and how they apply, by analogy, to all ecosystems.

Therefore, in conclusion, a few words about fish.

In 1957, down in the Appalachians near the Tennessee–North Carolina border, the U.S. Forest Service readied Abrams Creek for the impoundment of its lower reaches. Fontana Dam, when its gates closed across the Little Tennessee River, would raise the water level in the mouth of the creek. The stream's waters and any resident fish would become intermixed with the new reservoir's soon-to-be-stocked population of game fish. According to the logic of the time, Forest Service workers set about eliminating the stream species, or "rough" fish, as they were known in the terminology of the day.

Methodically, workers spread rotenone, a potent ichthyocide, into the clean, clear water of Abrams Creek. Hundreds of individual fish, representing dozens of species, floated motionless to the surface, gasping in their death throes. As the rotenone moved downstream, another phalanx of workers followed along, scooping up the dead and plopping them into jars of formaldehyde. Eventually the jars arrived at the National Museum of Natural History in Washington, D.C., to be catalogued by a member of the museum's ichthyological staff. In one of the jars the ichthyologist discovered a fish no biologist had previously seen. He named it *Noturus baileyi*, and it came to be known as the smoky madtom, a reference to its habitat in the Great Smoky Mountains. Because the only known population of smoky madtoms was found in Abrams Creek, and there were no records of this species from nearby streams, the newly discovered little catfish was assumed to be extinct. It would be nearly thirty years before that assumption was proven false.

Although I was only six when the smoky madtom was discovered, this fish and many others were to play a role in my development as a biologist, and to shape my ideas regarding ecosystems, species, and environmental protection. These notions lie at the foundation of the approach to orchid cultivation described in this book.

Noturus baileyi, the smoky madtom. Photo by J. R. Shute.

Official recognition that all species, not just the cute and cuddly ones, play a vital role in the pageant of life first arrived when Richard Nixon signed the Endangered Species Act into law on 3 February 1973. Passage of the act did more than focus public attention on the problem of biodiversity loss. Assigning a species to the endangered species list triggered a cascade of actions, among the most important of which was a stipulation that the government would develop a recovery plan for each listed species. Finding out what an endangered species needs in order to survive and recover requires research. The availability of money, in significant amounts for the first time, for field research on the ecology of the country's flora and fauna led many to pursue graduate studies in zoology, botany, or ecology.

One of those graduate students, eventually, was I. By the time I finally bumbled my way into a cadre of field biologists, nearly every American had heard of the Endangered Species Act, thanks to a charismatic, outspoken, and brilliant young University of Tennessee professor, David Etnier. Since arriving at the university, Etnier had set about filling the gaps in scientific knowledge about the most diverse freshwater fish fauna in the continental United States, that of Tennessee River and its watershed. By all accounts, he quickly became the most knowledgeable ichthyologist in the Southeast, and was soon to become the most famous in the country.

A 1973 duck hunt led Etnier (or "Ets," as friends call him) to the site of his most noteworthy discovery (Venable 1978). He found a spring feeding the Little Tennessee River, which led to the shoals above Coytee Springs. Etnier had not previously known there were shoals of this size in the lower reaches of the Little Tennessee. Moreover, this shoal would be flooded when the gates closed on the Tennessee Valley Authority's Tellico Dam, already under construction downstream. Ets resolved to revisit Coytee Springs during warmer weather.

On the morning of 12 August, the Little Tennessee was murky, obscuring Etnier's vision through his face mask as he snorkeled the Coytee Springs shoal. He saw only one fish. Thinking it was a sculpin, he poked at it with his finger. The fish shook its head but otherwise failed to respond. He poked again. Still, the mottled brown creature stood its ground, refusing to swim away. Ets scooped it up in his hands for a closer look. It was at this moment that humans first became aware of *Percina tanasi*, the snail darter.

Etnier clambered out of the river and called out to his friend Bob Stiles, a professor at Samford University in Birmingham, Alabama. The pair had been on an extended field trip, researching stream fish for several days. As they examined the new find, a local landowner sauntered up.

"Whatcha got?" he asked.

Etnier turned to face him. "Mister, this is a fish that will stop Tellico Dam."

Six years later the Supreme Court upheld a lower court's decision to halt the multibillion-dollar construction project because it would wipe out the entire population of snail darters at Coytee Springs, ruling that the fish was protected by the Endangered Species Act even from the actions of the federal government. An obscure, mud-colored, 3-inch fish became known from neighborhood taverns to the halls of the United States Congress. Under the leadership of Republican Senator Howard Baker of Tennessee, Congress subsequently acted to exempt the Tellico project from the Endangered Species Act. The Tennessee Valley Authority invested years of litigation and millions of dollars to have its way with the river. Today the waters of Tellico Lake have smothered the shoals at Coytee Springs.

Percina tanasi, the snail darter. Photo by J. R. Shute.

Other populations of snail darters were subsequently discovered, so the species has avoided extinction for now. It is no longer considered endangered, but the threat of extinction still looms, and the snail darter remains protected by the Endangered Species Act. The original population from Coytee Springs survives only in the genes of the descendants of a few fish, transplanted from the Little Tennessee to the nearby Hiwassee River in an early attempt to save them from presumed extinction. The rest of the famous Coytee Springs snail darters, like the shoal they inhabited since the Ice Age, were obliterated by the tide of development. The snail darter case proved that legislation even at the federal level does little to guarantee protection for our native plants and animals. What Congress giveth, Congress can easily taketh away.

By the Reagan era, environmentalists had begun to focus on the idea of harnessing market forces to achieve conservation goals. That trend may have developed as much out of frustration with Reagan's abysmally anticonservation Secretary of Interior, James Watt, as from a change in environmentalists' perception of the corporate community. With Watt a brick wall across the path to preservation, corporations became the only source of power that could be tapped to alter public policy. The idea became not to preserve biodiversity simply for the sake of its continued existence, but rather to justify saving species for economic reasons. If conservation could only be made profitable, it was reasoned, then an alternative to profit-generating, but unsustainable, development might be offered up. Environmentally concerned consumers would vote with their wallets. During the next fifteen years, projects sprang up all over the world to try to make conservation profitable (Dailey and Ellison 2002). In 1995 I became a part of one of these efforts, learning firsthand the realities of trying to harness the power of international markets for the benefit of the environment. Once again fish played a role, and by then Ets and I had become old friends.

In the early eighties, while I was teaching biology at the University of Tennessee, one of Ets' graduate students, Gerry Dinkins, discovered a new population of *Noturus baileyi* in Citico Creek in the Cherokee National Forest. There was a lot of excitement among field biologists, because, of course, this fish had supposedly become extinct some twenty-five years previously when Abrams Creek was poisoned. Because the only known populations of the smoky madtom were the one Dinkins found and the extinct one from Abrams Creek, the fish soon received designation as a federally endangered species, and research into its life cycle and the possibility of a recovery plan began.

In the mid 1980s, someone in Etnier's circle hit upon the idea of taking baby madtoms from Citico Creek, rearing them in aquariums, and relocating them to the site of their original discovery in Abrams Creek. A group of us set up a madtom hatchery in the animal maintenance facility at the University of Tennessee. Unfortunately, the hatchery was poorly installed and located in a windowless basement space harshly illuminated by industrial lighting. The prevailing environment affected nearly every habitat parameter needed for the baby catfishes to thrive. Constant noise, vibration, airborne contamination, and pathogens all reduced the survival rate. The first year, we ended up with three tiny fish to release into Abrams Creek, at a cost far greater than their equivalent weight in platinum. Obviously, we needed a better approach. By 1987 we thought we had the answer. Two more of Etnier's graduate students, husband and wife J. R. and Peggy Shute, along with myself and additional financial partners, founded an aquarium retail business. We envisioned the retail operation providing support for a small facility that would function as our madtom hatchery.

It almost worked. We ventured into Citico Creek in late spring. When we located a nest containing baby madtoms, we collected the tiny fish and brought them back to the hatchery facility. Records were maintained and surveys performed to ensure the removals were not negatively affecting the Citico Creek population. We learned, for example, that male fish robbed of their brood will spawn again, compensating for the loss of a few nests to the Abrams Creek project. We soon had scores of madtoms, and the cost of raising them had fallen to a fraction of that of the first year. The operation, however, needed to be larger, more efficient, and isolated from the tropical fish that were our prime retail product. The madtoms, after all, were denizens of a mountain stream. To maintain the annual cycle imposed upon them by millions of years of evolution, the fish needed a winter chilling. Otherwise, we would never be able to establish a captive breeding population, essential to producing the large number of madtoms required to restock Abrams Creek.

After a few seasons, the retail aquarium business was separated from the madtom hatchery, which became Conservation Fisheries, Incorporated (CFI), a nonprofit organization that continues to work on endangered fish recovery projects. Today, smoky madtoms again swim, feed, and reproduce in Abrams Creek—a perfect example of the value of creating a captive population rather than relying on natural reproductive rates.

Despite the time spent chasing madtoms, my major focus remained running the retail business. In addition to the usual pet store fish, our inventory included rare freshwater fish, marine fish, and delicate marine invertebrates. We knew that many of these species were harvested from their native habitats. As we gained experience in the aquarium business, we learned the extent of the damage done by those harvests. To sustain the demand for exotic pets, collectors were decimating acres of coral reef.

A smoky madtom rests on the bottom of its aquarium in the Conservation Fisheries hatchery. Photo by J. R. Shute.

The market for large, complex, and expensive marine aquariums blossomed in the 1980s owing to advances in filtration and lighting technology, as well as improved air shipping methods that for the first time made possible the reliable importation of delicate species from Southeast Asia. By the time the Clinton economic boom arrived in the early 1990s, the marine aquarium business was well established. Getting the fish from the ocean into the aquarium tanks of an eager public at the least possible cost became the aquarium industry's standard operating procedure.

Many coral reef fish are obtained for the aquarium trade using sodium cyanide, the same poison once used in the gas chamber. A fisherman sprays the poison into the spiky skeletal projections of the coral, where creatures such as the golden butterflyfish (*Chaetodon semilar-*

Chaetodon semilarvatus, the golden butterflyfish.

vatus) often congregate. Each coral polyp the cloud of sodium cyanide touches will eventually die. The fish, for their part, are stunned by the cyanide, making them easy to dislodge from the coral. Later, in a plastic bucket of fresh seawater, many of the fish recover from the initial effects of the cyanide and begin swimming around. Those that do not recover are tossed back into the water, to be eaten by other creatures, who in turn ingest a share of the cyanide.

Subsistence fishing equals survival in the areas of the Philippines, Indonesia, and elsewhere in the Indo-Pacific region where thousands of people live in appalling poverty. For each golden butterflyfish collected, a fisherman receives less than fifty cents. Within a week or two, the fish he collected will be swimming in a tank in an Atlanta shop, bearing a price more than three hundred times what he was paid. Meanwhile, a bacterial rot spreads across the coral where the polyps have been killed by the cyanide. About twenty years will be required for the coral head to completely recover. And the fisherman, endangered by his own crude equipment and the cyanide he must himself purchase, has little choice but to continue.

At its height, the trade in cyanide-caught fish removed millions of individual coral reef fish. Between the collector and the retailer, mortality approached 90 percent. Nevertheless, the trade has also generated millions of dollars in profits for importers in the United States, Europe, and Japan.

The web of interlocking business activity, official corruption, and callous disregard for the health of coral reefs constituting the aquarium cyanide trade presented an intimidating front in 1995 when I founded the American Marinelife Dealers Association (AMDA). Our objective was simple. We were out to convince the entire aquarium industry that the cyanide trade not only destroys coral reefs but also engenders a negative effect on retail sales. Fish captured with poisons and maintained under grossly suboptimal conditions between collection and retail sale almost always die in the hands of the hobby aquarist. Discouraged hobbyists give up, stop buying aquarium products, and find a different, presumably less challenging, leisure-time pursuit.

The AMDA set out to create a branding system to identify conscientious retailers who avoided the cyanide trade. We assumed that assuring hobbyists their fish had either been legally collected or properly reared in captivity would justify a greater cost. How wrong we were! A cacophony of strident opposition arose. Fish produced responsibly cost roughly twice as much as those plundered destructively, because the fishermen require more time to obtain the same catch. The technology needed to maintain fish awaiting sale also creates additional costs for exporters, importers, and retailers. Were suppliers willing to reduce profits to make room for these added expenses? Surely you jest.

Increases in the cost of doing business are inevitably passed along to the consumer. Were consumers willing to accept the added costs of a sustainable fishery? Only with independent assurances that the fish were indeed harvested and maintained appropriately. Since the mid 1990s the aquarium hobby industry has wrangled with certification. Initially developed by a coalition of aquarium industry stakeholders under the auspices of the U.S. branch of the World Wildlife Fund, the Marine Aquarium Council was created to certify that a given marine fish entered the aquarium trade cyanide-free. According to its Web site, the council as of 18 January 2003 has certified two collectors' associations, four exporters, five importers (three in the United States, one in Canada, and one in the Netherlands), and four U.S. retailers. The two collectors' associations represent a few dozen divers of the thousands working in the Philippines. Of the three U.S. importers, two not only actively supported the cyanide trade in the past but also vehemently opposed efforts to change it. At every step of the way the importers attempted to steer the nascent council toward a pro-industry interpretation of "sustainable" practices. To date, the Marine Aquarium Council's Web site describes certification as being in a "development phase" of unspecified duration. What is being developed, precisely, is unclear. No laboratory method yet exists to determine whether fish have been exposed to cyanide during the collection process.

The retail aquarium industry hardly rushed to seek certification, evidence against the notion that market forces can inevitably be harnessed to achieve desired environmental results. The current enrollment of retailers represents a mere 0.2 percent of U.S. aquarium dealers. Including even those dealers who say they *plan* to obtain certification but have not yet actually done so brings the total to fewer than a hundred companies worldwide, and raises the U.S.-only total to about 2.4 percent. Retailers have the greatest share of the responsibility for promoting certification, because they have direct contact with consumers making purchasing decisions. Because most retailers ignore the certification program, only the most environmentally aware hobbyists have even heard about it.

The Marine Aquarium Council provides a good example of "greenwashing." This neologism may be defined as carrying out all kinds of busy work, such as sponsoring an endless procession of conferences and issuing a tide of reports, while actually doing little to clean up environmental problems. Of the council's thirteen board members, six come from the aquarium industry, two represent consumers, and two come from South Pacific nongovernment organizations that survive by providing services for the council's overseas projects. Only three represent environmental organizations.

What does this series of fish anecdotes have to do with hardy orchids? Everything, if you share a desire to see wild orchid populations preserved and protected within the temperate zone. My ichthyological experiences reveal four facts about conservation as practiced in America:

1. The greatest threat to the planet's biodiversity comes from large-scale development.
2. Law alone is not enough to secure species protection.
3. Captive propagation is an essential element of species preservation and recovery of declining populations.
4. The marketplace cannot be expected to achieve the "right" answer to a given problem, only the most profitable one, absent some level of government regulation.

As my examples demonstrate, neither coercion by law nor tinkering with the marketplace much affects biodiversity preservation. On the other hand, giving people the tools and incentives to preserve habitat and species within their own communities does work. Fiji, where individual ownership of specific fishing grounds dictated by ancient local

Construction along Interstate 40 near Knoxville, Tennessee, typifies the most significant threat to native plants: habitat destruction.

The Farnham site on 29 April 2004.

traditions guides coral reef conservation, has thriving aquarium harvest and reef ecotourism industries, because wild fish collecting is well regulated and the fishing methods employed are sustainable. The reef remains pristine and draws many tourists. Tourists may return home and purchase an aquarium exhibiting Fijian fish.

In late April of 2004 I took my camera and drove out to the construction site that Bill Farnham had contacted me about in 2001. The little patch of piney woods and the orchids it sheltered had been altered beyond recognition. Yet Bill's lady's slippers bloomed in profusion under the white pine tree at my home. On the way back, a National Public Radio story reported that the administration of President George W. Bush had published new rules that would count captive-bred, hatchery populations of animal and plant species in determining the number of "wild" individuals in existence for purposes of determining status under the Endangered Species Act. Scientifically preposterous, and a perversion of Congress' original intent in creating the Endangered Species Act, these new rules could thwart all the good intentions of *ex situ* conservation efforts described in this book. I should like to close, therefore, with the emphatic assertion that no laboratory, no hatchery, and no greenhouse can substitute for an intact, unmolested habitat. *Ex situ* programs are a tool of conservation, not a substitute for any other approach.

Taxonomy of Hardy Orchid Genera

THIS TABLE IS BASED ON *Hardy Orchids* (Cribb and Bailes 1989) and *The Illustrated Encyclopedia of Orchids* (Pridgeon 1992), and includes every genus reported in these books as having at least some species that are potentially hardy in a frost-free alpine house. Most can be cultivated outdoors in much of the United States. Presumably these genera are in cultivation, at least in professional collections if not in the nursery trade. Not every genus in the table is described in this book. Readers with an interest in these genera should consult the references noted.

Despite the fact that orchid species names, and occasionally generic names, may change as a result of new discoveries about their relationships, horticulturists, even amateurs, should not eschew a working knowledge of orchid taxonomy. Genetic relationships may offer clues to cultural requirements shared among genera that otherwise appear quite disparate. With so many genera and species in the Orchidaceae, a taxonomic table such as this offers just about the only way to keep track.

Division Angiospermatophyta
Class Liliopsida
Superorder Lilianae
Order Liliales
Family Orchidaceae
Subfamily Apostaioideae (no hardy
   terrestrial species)
Subfamily Cypripedioideae
   Cypripedium
Subfamily Spiranthoideae
  Tribe Erythrodeae
    Subtribe Goodyerinae
     Goodyera
  Tribe Cranichidae
    Subtribe Spiranthinae
     Spiranthes
     Stenorrhynchus
Subfamily Orchidoideae
  Tribe Neottieae
    Subtribe Limodorinae
     Cephalanthera
     Epipactis
    Subtribe Listerineae
     Listera
     Neottia
  Tribe Diurideae
    Subtribe Chloraeineae
     Chloraea
    Subtribe Caladeniieae
     Caladenia
     Cyrtostylis
     Drakaea
     Elythranthera
    Subtribe Prasophyllineae
     Genoplesium
     Prasophyllum
    Subtribe Pterostyliidnae
     Pterostylis

    Subtribe Acianthinae
     Acianthus
     Corybus
    Subtribe Diuridineae
     Diuris
     Thelymitra
  Tribe Orchidieae
    Subtribe Orchidinae
     Aceras
     Amitostigma
     Anacamptis
     Barlia
     Coeloglossum
     Comperia
     Dactylorhiza
     Galearis
     Gymnadenia
     Himantoglossum
     Nigritella
     Ophrys
     Orchis
     Platanthera
     Ponerorchis
     Serapias
    Subtribe Habenariinae
     Habenaria
     Pecteilus
  Tribe Diseae
    Subtribe Disinae
     Disa
    Subtribe Coryciinae
     Disperis
    Subtribe Satyriinae
     Satyrium
Subfamily Epidendroideae
  Tribe Epidendreae
    Subtribe Laeliinae
     Epidendrum
     Encyclia

Tribe Vanilleae
  Subtribe Pogoniinae
    Pogonia
Tribe Arethuseae
  Subtribe Arethusinae
    Arethusa
  Subtribe Bletiinae
    Bletilla
    Calanthe
    Calopogon
Tribe Coelogyneae
  Subtribe Coelogyninae
    Pleione
Tribe Malaxideae
    Liparis
    Malaxis

Tribe Calypsoeae
    Calypso
    Dactylostalix
Tribe Epidendreae
  Subtribe Dendrobiinae
    Dendrobium
Subfamily Vandoideae
  Tribe Maxillarideae
    Subtribe Corallorhizinae
      Aplectrum
      Corallorhiza
      Cremastra
      Oreorchis
    Subtribe Cyrtopodiinae
      Cymbidium
      Cyrtopodium
      Dipodium

Orchid Selection Guide

THE FOLLOWING LISTS OF HARDY TERRESTRIAL ORCHIDS are provided to facilitate the creation of mixed plantings. Orchids are categorized according to their preferred placement in the garden and their season of bloom—two good places from which to start. Additional details, such as pH, bloom color, and hardiness, can be found in chapter 7. Please note that summer-dormant species are generally fall- to winter-blooming in North America.

Preferred Placement in the Garden

FULL SUN
Anacamptis pyramidalis
Arethusa bulbosa
Calopogon tuberosus
Epipactis gigantea
Epipactis helleborine
Platanthera blephariglottis
Platanthera ciliaris
Platanthera cristata

Platanthera integra
Platanthera integrilabia
Platanthera peramoena
Pogonia ophioglossoides
Spiranthes cernua var.
   odorata
Spiranthes spiralis
Thelymitra ixiodes

FULL SUN TO LIGHT SHADE
Gymnadenia conopsea
Ophrys apifera
Ophrys fusca
Ophrys holoserica
Ophrys insectifera
Ophrys lutea
Ophrys scolopax
Ophrys tenthredinifera

Ophrys vernixia
Orchis mascula
Orchis militaris
Orchis morio
Orchis purpurea
Orchis simia

FULL SUN TO PARTIAL SHADE

Bletilla Brigantes
Bletilla ochracea
Bletilla striata
Bletilla striata var. *alba*
Bletilla Yokohama
Spiranthes lacera
Spiranthes ochroleuca
Spiranthes sinensis
Spiranthes tuberosa
Spiranthes vernalis

PARTIAL SUN

Cymbidium faberi
Cymbidium floribundum
Cymbidium goeringii
Cymbidium kanran
Cypripedium japonicum
Disa uniflora
Eleorchis japonica
Pleione bulbocodioides
Spiranthes lucida

LIGHT SHADE TO FULL SUN

Dactylorhiza fuchsii
Thelymitra carnea
Thelymitra crinita
Thelymitra nuda

ALPINE GREENHOUSE

Calanthe alpina
Calanthe aristulifera

Calanthe discolor
Calanthe izu-insularis
Calanthe longicalcarata
Calanthe nipponica
Calanthe reflexa
Calanthe tricarinata
Disa uniflora

DAPPLED SHADE

Cypripedium acaule
Galearis spectabilis
Pleione formosana
Ponthieva racemosa

DAPPLED TO FULL SHADE

Goodyera pubescens
Goodyera repens

LIGHT SHADE

Dactylorhiza elata
Dactylorhiza maculata
Pleione Etna
Pleione forrestii
Pleione limprichtii
Pleione pleionoides
Pogonia japonica
Pterostylis alobula
Pterostylis banksii
Pterostylis baptistii
Pterostylis boormanii
Pterostylis concinna
Pterostylis cucullata
Pterostylis curta
Pterostylis grandiflora
Pterostylis longifolia
Pterostylis plumosa
Pterostylis rufa
Serapias lingua

PARTIAL SHADE

Caladenia caerulea
Caladenia carnea
Caladenia discoidea
Caladenia eminens
Cypripedium californicum
Cypripedium formosanum
Cypripedium kentuckiense
Cypripedium parviflorum
Cypripedium pubescens
Cypripedium reginae

PARTIAL TO FULL SHADE

Calypso bulbosa
Cypripedium montanum

SUMMER SHADE, WINTER SUN

Aplectrum hyemale
Tipularia discolor

SHADE

Liparis liliifolia
Platanthera flava
Platanthera grandiflora
Platanthera psycodes
Triphora trianthophora

Season of Bloom

EARLY SPRING

Aplectrum hyemale
Platanthera psycodes

SPRING

Bletilla Brigantes
Bletilla ochracea
Bletilla striata
Bletilla striata var. *alba*
Bletilla Yokohama

Calanthe aristulifera
Calanthe tricarinata
Cymbidium goeringii
Cypripedium acaule
Cypripedium formosanum
Cypripedium kentuckiense
Cypripedium parviflorum
Cypripedium pubescens
Cypripedium reginae
Eleorchis japonica
Galearis spectabilis
Gymnadenia conopsea
Platanthera grandiflora
Pleione bulbocodioides
Pleione Etna
Pleione formosana
Pleione forrestii
Pleione limprichtii
Pleione pleionoides
Thelymitra ixiodes

LATE SPRING
Cypripedium californicum
Cypripedium montanum
Dactylorhiza fuchsii
Pogonia japonica

LATE SPRING TO EARLY SUMMER
Cypripedium japonicum
Dactylorhiza elata
Dactylorhiza maculata

SPRING TO EARLY SUMMER
Thelymitra carnea
Thelymitra crinita
Thelymitra nuda

SPRING TO SUMMER
Calanthe alpina

Calanthe discolor
Calanthe izu-insularis
Calanthe longicalcarata
Spiranthes vernalis

SUMMER
Anacamptis pyramidalis
Arethusa bulbosa
Calopogon tuberosus
Epipactis gigantea
Epipactis helleborine
Liparis liliifolia
Platanthera ciliaris
Platanthera flava
Platanthera integra
Platanthera integrilabia
Pogonia ophioglossoides
Tipularia discolor
Triphora trianthophora

LATE SUMMER
Goodyera pubescens
Goodyera repens
Platanthera blephariglottis
Platanthera cristata
Platanthera peramoena
Spiranthes tuberosa

LATE SUMMER TO FROST
Spiranthes cernua var. odorata

FALL
Cymbidium floribundum
Ponthieva racemosa
Spiranthes lacera
Spiranthes lucida
Spiranthes ochroleuca
Spiranthes sinensis
Spiranthes spiralis

WINTER (SUMMER-DORMANT)
Caladenia caerulea
Caladenia carnea
Caladenia discoidea
Caladenia eminens
Calypso bulbosa
Disa uniflora
Ophrys apifera
Ophrys fusca
Ophrys holoserica
Ophrys insectifera
Ophrys lutea
Ophrys scolopax
Ophrys tenthredinifera
Ophrys vernixia
Orchis mascula
Orchis militaris
Orchis morio
Orchis purpurea
Orchis simia
Pterostylis alobula
Pterostylis banksii
Pterostylis baptistii
Pterostylis boormanii
Pterostylis concinna
Pterostylis cucullata
Pterostylis curta
Pterostylis grandiflora
Pterostylis longifolia
Pterostylis plumosa
Pterostylis rufa
Serapias lingua

VARIABLE
Calanthe nipponica
Calanthe reflexa
Cymbidium faberi
Cymbidium kanran

Suppliers and Organizations

U.S. SUPPLIERS

Cyp. Haven
2291 280th Street
Adel, Iowa 50003
(515) 993-4841
fax: (515) 993-3623
www.cyphaven.com

Species and hybrids of *Calopogon* and *Cypripedium*. Web site contains extensive cultural information on hardy orchids. Plant availability lists are posted in September for shipment the following winter. Contact Carson Whitlow at slipperguy@aol.com.

GroWild
7190 Hill Hughes Road
Fairview, Tennessee 37062
(615) 799-1910
fax: (615) 799-1912
www.growildnursery.com

Display garden includes orchids, but no plant offerings. Offers numerous species of southeastern native trees, shrubs, and perennials, including many rarities. Wholesale only but with an annual open house for retail customers. Contact Mike Berkley.

Hoosier Orchid Company
8440 West 82nd Street
Indianapolis, Indiana 46278
(317) 291-6269
fax: (317) 291-8949
www.hoosierorchid.com

Flasked germination and replate media. Also offers many tropical orchid species, but no hardy ones. Contact orchids@hoosierorchid.com.

Raising Rarities
P.O. Box 405
Jacksonville, Vermont 05342
(802) 368-7273 or (941) 697-5792
www.raisingrarities.com
   Cypripedium ×*andrewsii*, *C. Francis*, *C. kentuckiense*, *C. kentuckiense* × *C. speciosum*, *C. reginae*, and *C. reginae* f. *albolabium*. All species are seed grown and offered at blooming size. Contact Owen Robinson at orobinson@raisingrarities.com or Michael Jarrett at mjarrett@raisingrarities.com.

Red's Hardy Orchids
15920 Southwest Oberst Lane
Sherwood, Oregon 97140
(503) 625-6331
fax: (503) 625-8055
www.hardy-orchids.com
   Bletilla striata var. *alba*, *B. striata* var. *rosea*, *B.* Yokohama, *Calanthe reflexa*, *C. tricarinata*, *Cypripedium californicum* (seedlings), *Dactylorhiza fuchsii* (seedlings), *D. praetermissa* (seedlings), *D. purpurella* (seedlings), *Orchis mascula*, and *Pleione* (numerous species, hybrids, and cultivars). Sometimes also offers Asian cypripediums. All plants are nursery propagated. Contact Dick Cavender at red@hardy-orchids.com.

Roberts Flower Supply
12390 Root Road
Columbia Station, Ohio 44028
(440) 236-5571
www.orchidmix.com

More than twenty species of *Cypripedium* from Asia, Europe, and North America, all seed grown. Visit the Web site to view photographs and ordering information. Also offers a wide variety of orchid supplies, including a potting mix for cypripediums. Contact rfs@orchidmix.com.

Rocky Mountain Orchids
P.O. Box 105
Bigfork, Montana 59911
(406) 837-5285
fax: (406) 837-6441
www.rmorchids.com
   Cypripedium montanum, *C. pubescens*, and *C. reginae*. Plants are offered from seedling to blooming size. Contact Rodd May at RMO@centurytel.net.

Shooting Star Nursery
444 Bates Road
Frankfort, Kentucky 40601
(502) 223-1679
fax: (502) 227-5700
www.shootingstarnursery.com
   Seedlings of *Cypripedium kentuckiense*, *C. pubescens*, *C. reginae*, and many other species native to eastern North America. All are nursery propagated. Contact Marianne Hunt at shootingstarnursery@msn.com.

Spangle Creek Labs
21950 County Road 445
Bovey, Minnesota 55709
(218) 247-0245
www.uslink.net/~scl/index.html

Seedlings of *Cypripedium candidum, C. guttatum, C. kentuckiense, C. parviflorum, C. pubescens,* and *C. reginae.* Extensive cultural advice and assistance offered through the Web site. Contact Bill and Carol Steele at carolscl@uslink.net.

Sunshine Farm and Gardens
HC 67 Box 539B
Renick, West Virginia 24966
(304) 497-2208
fax: (304) 497-2698
www.sunfarm.com
   Aplectrum hyemale, Goodyera pubescens, Spiranthes cernua var. *odorata* 'Chadd's Ford', *Tipularia discolor,* and hundreds of other native and exotic perennials. All are nursery propagated. Contact Barry Glick at barry@sunfarm.com.

Van Bourgondien
245 Route 109
P.O. Box 1000
Babylon, New York 11702
(800) 622-9997
www.dutchbulbs.com
   Bletilla ochracea (identified as *B. striata aurea*), *B. striata, B. striata* var. *alba, Cypripedium* species, and *Pecteilis radiata* (identified as *Habenaria radiata*). This large, traditional mail-order bulb company usually offers a few orchid species each year. Contact blooms@dutchbulbs.com.

Vermont Ladyslipper Company
56 Leduc Road
New Haven, Vermont 05472

www.vtladyslipper.com
   Cypripedium acaule, C. ×andrewsii, C. parviflorum, C. pubescens, and *C. reginae.* This seed laboratory and nursery sells only propagated *Cypripedium* species and hybrids, blooming size and smaller. Contact Scott and Ellen Durkee at vtlsc@together.net.

OTHER SUPPLIERS

Importation of orchid plants into the United States requires a permit from the USDA and a phytosanitary certificate from the country of origin. Most suppliers are familiar with these regulations and are glad to assist with the necessary paperwork, although they usually assess a small fee for the trouble. For specific advice on importing plants from abroad, visit orchidweb.org/permits.html and orchidweb.org/orchids/culture/importing.pdf.

Fraser's Thimble Farms
175 Arbutus Road
Salt Spring Island
V8K 1A3 British Columbia
Canada
www.thimblefarms.com
   Numerous species and hybrids, including *Anacamptis, Aplectrum, Bletilla, Calanthe, Calopogon, Calypso, Cephalanthera, Cypripedium, Dactylorhiza, Eleorchis, Epipactis, Goodyera, Gymnadenia, Ophrys, Orchis, Platanthera, Pleione, Ponerorchis,* and *Spiranthes.*

My Orchids
Heinrich Beyrle
Postfach 1129
86316 Friedberg
Germany
www.myorchids.de

Numerous species and hybrids of *Anacamptis*, *Caladenia*, *Chiloglottis*, *Dactylorhiza*, *Disa*, *Diuris*, *Ophrys*, *Orchis*, *Pleione*, *Pogonia*, *Pterostylis*, *Satyrium*, *Serapias*, *Serapicamptis*, and *Thelymitra*. All plants are nursery propagated using mycorrhizal fungi. The Web site offers exceptionally detailed and clearly written cultural instructions (in both German and English) for the genera offered, together with references and color photos—a must-visit site!

Paul Christian Rare Plants
P.O. Box 468
Wrexham LL13 9XR
United Kingdom
www.rareplants.co.uk

A large variety of hardy terrestrial orchid species and hybrids, all nursery propagated. Mail order only.

ORGANIZATIONS

American Horticultural Society
7931 East Boulevard Drive
Alexandria, Virginia 22308
(703) 768-5700
www.ahs.org

American Orchid Society
16700 AOS Lane
Delray Beach, Florida 33446
(877) 672-4437
www.aos.org

National Wildflower Research Center
2600 FM 973 North
Austin, Texas 78725
(512) 929-3600

New England Wildflower Society
Garden in the Woods
180 Hemenway Road
Framingham, Massachusetts 01701
www.newfs.org

More than two hundred species, including several orchids. Sells seeds and publishes a list of sustainable native plant sources. Contact Bill Cullina at cullina@newfs.org.

North American Native Orchid
  Alliance
P.O. Box 772121
Ocala, Florida 34477
www.naorchid.org

Conversion Tables

INCHES	CENTIMETERS	FEET	METERS
1/4	0.6	1	0.3
1/2	1.25	6	1.8
1	2.5	8	2.4
2	5.0	10	3.0
3	7.5	20	6.0
4	10	25	7.5
5	12.5	30	9.0
6	15	50	15
7	18	100	30
8	20	1000	300
9	23	2500	750
10	25	5000	1500
15	37	7500	2250
20	51	10,000	3000

$$°C = 5/9 \times (°F - 32)$$
$$°F = (9/5 \times °C) + 32$$

USDA Hardiness Zone Map

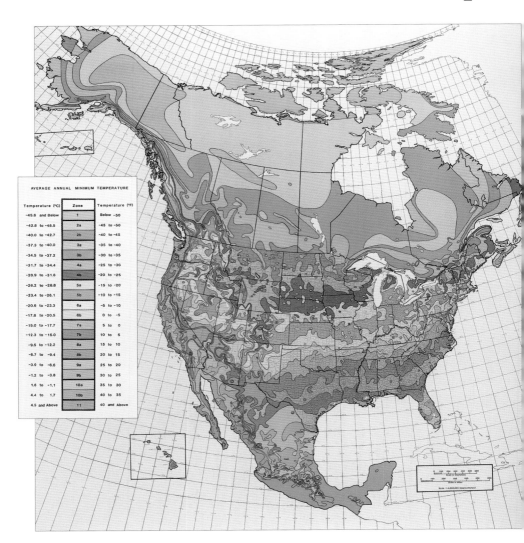

AVERAGE ANNUAL MINIMUM TEMPERATURE

Temperature (°C)	Zone	Temperature (°F)
-45.6 and Below	1	Below -50
-42.8 to -45.5	2a	-45 to -50
-40.0 to -42.7	2b	-40 to -45
-37.3 to -40.0	3a	-35 to -40
-34.5 to -37.2	3b	-30 to -35
-31.7 to -34.4	4a	-25 to -30
-28.9 to -31.6	4b	-20 to -25
-26.2 to -28.8	5a	-15 to -20
-23.4 to -26.1	5b	-10 to -15
-20.6 to -23.3	6a	-5 to -10
-17.8 to -20.5	6b	0 to -5
-15.0 to -17.7	7a	5 to 0
-12.3 to -15.0	7b	10 to 5
-9.5 to -12.2	8a	15 to 10
-6.7 to -9.4	8b	20 to 15
-3.9 to -6.6	9a	25 to 20
-1.2 to -3.8	9b	30 to 25
1.6 to -1.1	10a	35 to 30
4.4 to 1.7	10b	40 to 35
4.5 and Above	11	40 and Above

Bibliography

Anderson, Allen. 1996. "The Reintroduction of *Platanthera ciliaris* in Canada." In *North American Native Terrestrial Orchids: Propagation and Production*. Ed. Carol Allen. Conference Proceedings, North American Native Terrestrial Orchid Conference, 16–17 March 1996. 73–76.

Bentley, Stanley L. 2000. *Native Orchids of the Southern Appalachian Mountains*. Chapel Hill: University of North Carolina Press.

Beyrle, Heinrich. 2003. "My Orchids." http://www.myorchids.de.

Brown, Paul Martin. 1997. *Wild Orchids of the Northeastern United States*. Ithaca, New York: Cornell University Press.

———. 2002. *Wild Orchids of Florida*. Gainesville: University of Florida Press.

Brumbeck, William. 1988. "Collection of Plants From the Wild: One Propagator's View." *Wildflower* (Spring).

Campbell, Faith T. 1988. "Boycotting the Wild Plant Trade." *Garden* (January/February).

Cavender, Dick. 2002. "Hardy Terrestrial Orchids." http://www.hardy-orchids.com/orchids.html.

Christian, Paul. 2003. "Paul Christian Rare Plants." http://rareplants.co.uk/index.htm.

Chu, Chin-Chang, and Kenneth W. Mudge. 1996. "Propagation and Conservation of Native Lady's Slipper Orchids (*Cypripedium acaule*, *C. calceolus*, and *C. reginae*)." In *North American Native Terrestrial Orchids: Propagation and Production*. Ed. Carol Allen. Conference Proceedings, North American Native Terrestrial Orchid Conference, 16–17 March 1996. 107–112.

Clausen, Ruth Rogers, and Nicholas H. Ekstrom. 1989. *Perennials for American Gardens*. New York: Random House.

Coleman, Ronald A. 1995. *The Wild Orchids of California*. Ithaca, New York: Cornell University Press.

——. 2002. *The Wild Orchids of Arizona and New Mexico*. Ithaca, New York: Cornell University Press.

Cribb, Phillip. 1992. *Orchids: A Romantic History with a Guide to Cultivation*. London: Inklink.

——. 1997. *The Genus Cypripedium*. Portland, Oregon: Timber Press.

Cribb, Phillip, and Christopher Bailes. 1989. *Hardy Orchids*. Portland, Oregon: Timber Press.

Cribb, Phillip J., Mark W. Chase, and Finn N. Rasmussen. 1999. *Genera Orchidacearum*. Vol. 1. Oxford: Oxford University Press.

——. 2001. *Genera Orchidacearum*. Vol. 2. Oxford: Oxford University Press.

Cullina, William. 2000. *The New England Wildflower Society Guide to Growing and Propagating Wildflowers of the United States and Canada*. New York: Houghton Mifflin.

Daily, Gretchen C., and Katherine Ellison. 2002. *The New Economy of Nature: The Quest to Make Conservation Profitable*. Washington, D.C.: Island Press.

Darnell, A. W. 1976. *Orchids for the Outdoor Garden*. Ashford, England: L. Reeve, 1930. Reprint, Dover Publications.

Druse, Ken. 1992. *The Natural Shade Garden*. New York: Clarkson-Potter.

Durkee, Scott. 2000. "*Cypripedium acaule* and *Cypripedium reginae*: Successful Cultivation of Two North American Lady's Slipper Orchids." *Orchids* 69 (9), September: 864–869.

Fanfani, Alberto, and Walter Rossi. 1988. *Guide to Orchids*. New York: Simon and Schuster.

Fraser, Richard, and Nancy Fraser. 2003. "Hardy Orchids." http://www.thimblefarms.com/98orchidtf.html.

Gill, Douglas E. 1996. "The Natural Population Ecology of Temperate Terrestrials." In *North American Native Terrestrial Orchids: Propagation and Production*. Ed. Carol Allen. Conference Proceedings, North American Native Terrestrial Orchid Conference, 16–17 March 1996. 91–106.

Ginsburg, Elisabeth. 2004. "Got Five Years? You Might Grow a Lady-Slipper." *The New York Times*, 14 March 2004.

Glick, Barry. 1995. "A Garden-Friendly Native Orchid." *Plants and Gardens News* (Spring): 8–9.

——. 2000. "Sunshine Farm and Gardens." http://www.sunfarm.com/.

Griesback, P., and J. Asker. 1983. "Orchids of the Boundary Waters Canoe Area of Northern Minnesota." In *North American Terrestrial Orchid Symposium*. Ed. E. H. Plaxton. Michigan Orchid Society.

Gupton, Oscar W., and Fred Swope. 1986. *Wild Orchids of the Middle Atlantic States*. Knoxville: University of Tennessee Press.

Hansen, Eric. 2000. *Orchid Fever*. New York: Pantheon Press. 243.

Holman, R. T. 1976. "Cultivation of *Cypripedium calceolus* and *Cypripedium reginae*." *American Orchid Society Bulletin* 45: 415.

Horticulture. 2000. "Field Notes, Southeast: Lady's Slippers for Everyone." *Horticulture* (March).

Hunter, Margie. 2002. *Gardening with the Native Plants of Tennessee: The Spirit of Place*. Knoxville: University of Tennessee Press.

Hutson, Robert W., William F. Hutson, and Aaron J. Sharp. 1995. *Great Smoky Mountain Wildflowers*. Northbrook, Illinois: Windy Pines.

Jones, Samuel B., Jr., and Leonard Foote. 1990. *Gardening with Native Wildflowers*. Portland, Oregon: Timber Press.

Justice, William S., and C. Ritchie Bell. 1968. *Wildflowers of North Carolina*. Chapel Hill: University of North Carolina Press.

Keenan, Philip E. 2001. "Conservation Musings." *Orchids* 70 (2), February: 124–128.

Lehmberg, Verne. 2002. "Deception in the Acid Bogs." *Orchids* 71 (2), February: 138–146.

Liggio, Joe, and Ann Orto Liggio. 1999. *Wild Orchids of Texas*. Austin: University of Texas Press.

Light, Marilyn. 1996. "Reproductive Constraints in *Cypripedium*: Horticultural and Conservation Viewpoints." In *North American Native Terrestrial Orchids: Propagation and Production*. Ed. Carol Allen. Conference Proceedings, North American Native Terrestrial Orchid Conference, 16–17 March 1996. 77–90.

Malmgren, Svante. 1996. "Orchid Propagation: Theory and Practice." In *North American Native Terrestrial Orchids: Propagation and Production*. Ed. Carol Allen. Conference Proceedings, North American Native Terrestrial Orchid Conference, 16–17 March 1996. 63–72.

May, Rodd, and Karen May. 2002. "Growing Two Lady's-Slipper Orchids." *Orchids* 71 (1), January: 22–26.

Myers, Robert F. 1989. *Micronesian Reef Fishes*. Barrigada, Guam: Coral Graphics.

National Wildflower Research Center. 1989. *Wildflower Handbook*. Austin: Texas Monthly Press.

Neptune, Wilford B. 1999. "Growing Native North American Orchids." *Orchids* 68 (3), March: 230–235.

Nolt, John, Athena Lee Bradley, Mike Knapp, Donald Earl Lampard, and Jonathan Scherch. 1997. *What Have We Done?: The Foundation for Global Sustainability's State of the Bioregion Report for the Upper Tennessee Valley and the Southern Appalachian Mountains*. Washburn, Tennessee: Earth Knows Publications.

Orchard, Walter. 2000. "Disas." *Orchids* 69 (7), July: 634–644.

Orleans, Susan. 1998. *The Orchid Thief*. New York: Ballantine.

Phillips, Harry R. 1985. *Growing and Propagating Wildflowers*. Chapel Hill: University of North Carolina Press.

Plummer, Nicholas W. 2000. "*Cypripedium parviflorum*: A Terrestrial Orchid to Grow on the Windowsill." *Orchids* 69 (9), September: 870–874.

Pridgeon, Alec M. 1992. *The Illustrated Encyclopedia of Orchids*. Portland, Oregon: Timber Press.

Quammen, David. 2000. *The Boilerplate Rhino: Nature in the Eye of the Beholder*. New York: Scribner.

Rafinesque, C. S. 1828. *Medical Flora; or Manual of the Medical Botany of the United States of North America*. Philadelphia: Atkinson and Alexander.

Riley, Clark T. 1999. "Hardy Bletillas." http://www.orchidmall.com/general/bletilla.htm.

Seviak, C. 1983. "U.S. Terrestrial Orchids: Patterns and Problems." In *North American Terrestrial Orchid Symposium*. Ed. E. H. Plaxton. Michigan Orchid Society.

Smith, Richard M. 1998. *Wildflowers of the Southern Mountains*. Knoxville: University of Tennessee Press.

Smith, Welby R. 1993. *Orchids of Minnesota*. Minneapolis: University of Minnesota Press.

Steele, William K. 1996. "Large-Scale Production of North American *Cypripedium* Species." In *North American Native Terrestrial Orchids: Propagation and Production*. Ed. Carol Allen. Conference Proceedings, North American Native Terrestrial Orchid Conference, 16–17 March 1996. 11–26.

Stewart, Scott L. 2002. "Saving a Native Orchid." *Orchids* 71 (10), October: 916–919.

Still, Steven M. 1994. *Manual of Herbaceous Ornamental Plants*. Champaign, Illinois: Stipes.

Stokes, Donald, and Lillian Stokes. 1992. *Stokes Wildflower Book*. New York: Little, Brown.

Stoutamire, Warren. 1996. "Seeds and Seedlings of *Platanthera leucophaea* (Orchidaceae)." In *North American Native Terrestrial Orchids: Propagation and Production*. Ed. Carol Allen. Conference Proceedings, North American Native Terrestrial Orchid Conference, 16–17 March 1996. 55–62.

Stupka, Arthur. 1965. *Wildflowers in Color*. New York: HarperCollins.

Taylor, D. L., and T. D. Bruns. 1999. "Population, Habitat and Genetic Correlates of Mycorrhizal Specialization in the 'Cheating' Orchids *Corallorhiza maculata* and *C. mertensiana*." *Molecular Ecology* 8 (10): 1719–1732.

Tennessee, State of. 1985. "The Rare Plant Protection and Conservation Act of 1985." *Tennessee Code Annotated*. Section 70-8-301-314.

——. 2003. "Rare Plant Protection and Conservation Regulations." http://www.state.tn.us/sos/rules/0400/0400-06/0400-06-02.pdf.

Tennessee Department of Agriculture. 2003. "Rules of Tennessee Department of Agriculture, Division of Plant Industries." http://www.state.tn.us/sos/rules/0080/0080-06/0080-06-21.pdf.

Tennessee Department of Environment and Conservation. 2003. "Environmental Permits Handbook." http://www.state.tn.us/environment/permits/enddeal.php.

Tullock, John H. 1997. *Natural Reef Aquariums*. Shelburne, Vermont: Microcosm.

——. 2002. "Orchids Outdoors." *Orchids* 71 (5), May: 422–427.

Turkel, Marnie. 2002. "Growing *Pleione formosana*." *Orchids* 71 (12), December: 1108–1109.

U. S. Department of Agriculture, Natural Resources Conservation Service. 1999. "State Rankings by Acreage and Rate of Non-Federal Land Developed." http://www.nhq.nrcs.usda.gov/CCS/devtable.html.

Venable, Sam. 1978. "Mister, This Fish Will Stop Tellico." *The Knoxville News-Sentinel*, 18 June 1978.

Waskowski, Sally, and Andy Waskowski. 1994. *Gardening with Native Plants of the South*. Dallas, Texas: Taylor.

Whitlow, Carson. 1996. "Mass Production of *Calopogon tuberosus*." In *North American Native Terrestrial Orchids: Propagation and Production*. Ed. Carol Allen. Conference Proceedings, North American Native Terrestrial Orchid Conference, 16–17 March 1996. 5–10.

——. 2003. "Cyp. Haven." http://www.cyphaven.com.

Yanetti, Robert. 1996. "*Arethusa bulbosa* Life Cycle, Propagation and Production." In *North American Native Terrestrial Orchids: Propagation and Production*. Ed. Carol Allen. Conference Proceedings, North American Native Terrestrial Orchid Conference, 16–17 March 1996. 27–42.

de Zacks, Renate L. 1999. "Cooking Up Conservation." *Orchids* 68 (4), April: 368–377.

Zettler, Lawrence W. 1996. "Symbiotic Seed Germination of Terrestrial Orchids in North America during the Last Decade: A Progress Report." In *North American Native Terrestrial Orchids: Propagation and Production*. Ed. Carol Allen. Conference Proceedings, North American Native Terrestrial Orchid Conference, 16–17 March 1996. 43–54.

——. 1999. "Orchids Go Native." *Orchids* 68 (1), January: 14–21.

Index